What's True About Christianity?

An Introduction to Christian Faith and Practice

What's True about Christianity?

An Introduction to Christian Faith and Practice

Don Thorsen

THE HEART OF THE MATTER 1

What's True about Christianity?
An Introduction to Christian Faith and Practice
©2020 Claremont Press
1235 N. College Ave.
Claremont, CA 91711

ISBN 978-1-946230-40-9 (print)
     978-1-946230-42-3 (ebook)

Library of Congress Cataloging-in-Publication Data

What's True about Christianity? An Introduction to Christian Faith
and Practice / Don Thorsen
        xiv + 213 pp. 22 x 15 cm. –(The Heart of the Matter 1)
        Includes indices.
        ISBN   978-1-946230-41-6 (print)
               978-1-946230-42-3 (ebook)

        1. Theology, Doctrinal Popular works. **2.** Christian life.
        3. Christianity Essence, genius, nature.

        BT77 .T467 2020

In loving memory of my brother
Norman Thorsen

Contents

Part Five
"So That Whosoever Believes in Him Should Not Perish"

Part Six
"But May Have Eternal Life"

Editor's Preface

The lives of theologians, Biblical scholars and similar religious studies scholars are odd. Most such scholars enter into the profession because they believe that truth matters and that there is great value in doggedly pursuing truth and in sharing the results of that pursuit with communities of faith. However, most of these scholars practice their truth-seeking vocation in the professional setting of higher education where they serve as college, university and seminary professors. Almost without exception, the spoken and unspoken strictures of the academic world leave these religious studies scholars — like all scholars — feeling pressured to write and publish in academic journals and scholarly book series. This academic pressure to publish only in the most exclusive and prestigious forums typically results in a greatly diminished readership for these scholars' literary output.

In the meantime, while religious studies scholars are busy producing tomes for a few dozen scholars who happen to share their particular expertise, millions of reflection-hungry persons of faith struggle to find mature and critically engaged religious studies content to meet their own needs for insight and growth. The cultural pattern is clear: Scholars write for scholars. Critically minded non-specialists are left to their own devices. Engagement with the reading public is not a part of the scholarly mission. Wordsmithing for those outside the guild of religious studies scholarship is left to popular writers with less training, less expertise and often less insight.

This series is designed to free scholars to write outside the artificial constraints which too commonly separate the scholar and the saint. In this series, we are inviting seasoned scholars to write for the masses. We invite these scholars to write about what they care about, to write in the idioms of their everyday lives and to write for the reflective non-specialist. This series is designed to connect the scholar with the saint in pursuit of accessible insight.

--Thomas E. Phillips, editor

Forward and Acknowledgements

What do you think of when you see "John 3:16"?
Our modern world is scattered with this particular sequence of words and numbers. We see it on billboards next to giant pictures of the Bible. We see it on neon picket signs in city squares. We see it on the bottom of our yellow shopping bags, and on the inner lining of the bottom of a soda cup. We see it on television and on the poster boards of strangers at sporting events. It's tattooed on the person standing in front of us in line to get coffee in the morning. It's graffitied on the wall by the freeway.

What does this strange sequence of words and numbers bring to mind? Does the phrase "John 3:16" remind you of your best days in Vacation Bible School, or does it remind you of times you have felt rejected or shut out by Christians? Do you even know what this phrase means at all?

For better or for worse, John 3:16 has become one of the most recognizable phrases in the world. Somehow, this verse from the Bible became the most common representation of Christianity. But how often do we actually reflect on what this verse means?

John 3:16

John 3:16 may be the best verse in the Bible — or Scripture — with which to begin learning about Jesus Christ and Christianity. However, if you get no further than John 3:16, then you'll have both an inadequate and misleading view of the verse as well as of Jesus and Christianity.

John 3:16 says: "For God so loved the world that he gave his only son [Jesus] so that everyone who believes in him may not perish but may have eternal life." In order to understand this verse, it is important to interpret John 3:16 in its historical and literary context. But at first glance, it's not difficult to understand why the verse is popular: It talks about love, belief, and eternal life!

People unfamiliar with Christianity often know, at least, about John 3:16. Who hasn't seen the biblical reference plastered on a sign, and held up at a professional sporting event? As television cameras pan across football, basketball, and other sporting events, it's not uncommon to see a fan holding up sign that reads: John 3:16. So, what's the big deal?

Even people who are familiar with John 3:16 may have muddled opinions about it. For some, the verse is essential for bringing people to believe in Jesus Christ and the point of evangelistic decision. For other people, John 3:16 is thought to emphasize too narrow a view of conversion, which does not represent the spiritual journey of the majority of Christians around the world. For still others, the verse is thought to marginalize and discriminate against Christians who don't fit into a particular mold of Christian belief, value, and practice.

Despite differing opinions, John 3:16 remains important for a variety of reasons. First, it helps non-Christians to learn basic biblical teachings about Jesus, the eternal life he proclaimed, and the benefits people consequently experience in life here and now. Second, the study of John 3:16 may help to bring greater unity among Christians in their understanding of Jesus' "gospel" (from Greek *euangelion*, "good news, good story"). Third, John 3:16 represents a starting point for learning about the breadth and depth of what Scripture has to say to everyone in the world—non-Christians and Christians, East and West, South and North. Although the gospel of Jesus occurred in a particular place and time, it is intended for people at all times and places.

Themes

I think that John 3:16 includes some themes that need discussing. These themes do not derive directly from the verse, but John 3:16 implies them. In order to know more about the verse, as well as about Jesus and Christianity, I have taken parts of John 3:16, and then used them as section headings for this book.

Part 1 of this book looks at John 3:16 in its context. After that, I have included five additional sections, which divide the verse in five parts. Part 2 is entitled "For God so loved the world," and it has to do with who God is. Part 3 is entitled "The world," and it has to do with the nature of the world and of people. Part 4 is entitled "That he gave his only son," and it has to do with who Jesus is. Part 5 is entitled "So that everyone who believes in him may not perish," and it has to do with the nature of salvation and of the Christian life. Part 6 is entitled "But may have eternal life," and it has to do with future life to come. This book is not intended to present the whole of Christian beliefs, values, and practices. Instead, it introduces some of the most crucial teachings found in Scripture. Thus, John 3:16 serves as a perfect starting point for learning about Jesus and Christianity.

Some might call this a book of theology, since it talks about God. After all, *theology* derives from the Greek words for "God" (*theos*) and "word, reason, study" (*logos*). Others might call it apologetics, since it gives an explanation or defense of Christianity. *Apologetics* derives from the Greek word for "defense, apology" (*apologia*). Technically, both are correct, since I talk about God and about reasons for Christians' belief, for their hope, and for their love. I talk about belief, hope, and love because often people in general and Christians in particular focus only on beliefs. Too many think that having right beliefs or right ideas is sufficient for rightly understanding God and Scripture. However, Christianity has more to do with a right and loving relationship with God than with right propositional claims. It has more to do with hope for eternal life than with rational and empirical claims to certainty, and Christianity has more to do with loving our neighbors as ourselves — spiritually and physically, individually and collectively, righteously and justly. Having faith alone, or right belief alone, is not the whole of Christianity. On the contrary, it has more to do with our relationship with God, which affects our hopes and loves as well as our beliefs. In addition to our relationship and love for God, Christianity has to do our relationship with others, whom we are to love as we love ourselves. Thus, this book introduces some of the most crucial teachings found in Scripture, and how they inform Christian belief, hope, and love.

Acknowledgements

I want to thank my three daughters — Liesl, Heidi, and Dana — for their ongoing love and support of me in my writing. I'm also thankful to my sons-in-law: Lucas Porter, who is married to Liesl, and Will Oxford, who is married to Heidi. In addition, I want to thank Heidi for reading, editing, and contributing to my final manuscript. Her input was invaluable to me.

Kathy Armistead was especially helpful to me throughout the writing process, encouraging as well as advising me. John Trent also provided guidance that helped me in publishing the book.

Finally, I'm indebted to my brother Norman, who passed away too early in life. He was a good friend, as well as brother, and it is in his memory that I dedicate this book.

Part One

John 3:16

All Are Welcome!

Two thousand years ago, in a dry and dusty part of the world, there was a man named Nicodemus. Nicodemus was a leader in his community, which sought to uphold and protect its unique culture and tradition in a world that was always changing. Empires would rise and fall, but this community would remain. Nevertheless, this community (like so many communities) was resistant to change. So, when a new person showed up in town doing miraculous things and spreading teachings like no one ever heard before, Nicodemus decided to learn more. One evening Nicodemus set out alone, after the sky turned dark and the air turned cool, and he went to find this man.

So many people know the verse John 3:16, but fewer know about Nicodemus. He was a member of the Pharisee school of thought, and also served on the Sanhedrin, which was an assembly of Jewish leaders with political as well as religious authority. So, it is noteworthy that Nicodemus sought Jesus.

Nicodemus visited Jesus at night, which has led Christians throughout the centuries to question Nicodemus's intentions. Why did he come at night? Was Nicodemus afraid? What was he afraid of: Personal ridicule? Religious shunning? Political ruin? Violent retaliation? After all, Jesus had been a political activist as well as a religious leader. In the chapter preceding John 3, John—the purported author of the book of John—tells about Jesus using a whip of cords to drive money changers out of the Jewish temple, overturning tables, and spilling money out on the ground (John 2:13-22). This so-called "cleansing" of the temple was more than a religious act; it defied the social, political, and economic structures of ancient Israel.

Nicodemus may also have come to Jesus as a spokesperson on behalf of others. In John 3:2, Nicodemus says, "Rabbi, we know that you are a teacher…" See also Jesus' responses to Nicodemus, using the plural form of "you" in the original Greek language in which this part of Scripture was written (vv. 7, 11, 12). Regardless of

3

whether Nicodemus spoke for himself or on behalf of others, questions have persisted with regard to why he came at night.

Too often I have heard preachers and read biblical commentators that criticized Nicodemus for coming at night, and yet Jesus welcomed him. Jesus welcomed him! John does not give evidence that Jesus was critical of Nicodemus's visit. On the contrary, the two men engaged in a lively conversation that resulted in some of the most memorable words spoken by Jesus.

It is likely that Nicodemus came to praise Jesus, describing him as a teacher who had come from God, noting that Jesus performed signs that confirmed God's presence. It is not clear how knowledgeably or wholeheartedly Nicodemus made these claims. In any case, Jesus was quick to change the subject. Jesus didn't want to talk about signs and miracles, but rather the profound spiritual matters pertaining to his gospel message. Jesus did not question Nicodemus's intentions about why or when he had come. Jesus welcomed him! Nicodemus probably could have come to meet Jesus in any place, at any time, and with the shabbiest of intentions, and Jesus would have welcomed him.

Jesus Welcomed Everyone

Throughout Scripture, Jesus repeatedly welcomed people, including those who were ostracized in society—ostracized for spiritual as well as for physical, social, and cultural reasons. Let us first consider those ostracized for religious reasons. Jesus welcomed sinners. For example, he did not condemn a woman caught in adultery, who had been brought to Jesus by a vengeful crowd (John 8:1-11). (Unfairly, only an adulterous woman was brought, but not also the adulterous man.) Jesus also told parables about welcoming sinners, such as, welcoming a prodigal son who had wantonly wasted his father's inheritance (Luke 15:11-32).

Now let us consider those ostracized for physical, social, and cultural reasons, and not because they were sinners. Most notably, Jesus said that he fulfilled prophesies in Isaiah because he came to bring good news to the poor, proclaim release to captives, heal the blind, and let those oppressed go free (Luke 4:16-21). These are people who suffered, not necessarily because of sin, but also because of physical, social, and cultural causes. Jesus welcomed the poor, crippled, and blind, who were social outcasts (Luke 12:33; cf.

4

14:12-14). He welcomed women, who were marginalized in society, such as the Samaritan woman at the well (John 4:1-42). Jesus welcomed tax collectors, who were considered economic and political oppressors, such as Zacchaeus (Luke 19:1-10). Jesus welcomed — and even praised — those who were not of the Jewish religion: Roman centurion (Luke 7:1-10), Canaanite woman from Syrophonecia (Matthew 15:21-28), and Samaritans, who were thought to be cultish heretics as well as ethnic half-breeds (Luke 17:11-19). He welcomed Nicodemus, who represented both the religious and political leadership of Israel (John 3:1-17). Jesus even said that we are to love our enemies, and to pray for them (Matthew 5:43-44). So, if there is a message to be learned about Jesus' encounter with Nicodemus, it is that all are welcome to come to him.

Why People Feel Unwelcome

Why is it that Christianity so often is known for being unwelcoming, judgmental, and discriminatory? A common anecdote is that people like Jesus, but not his "fan club." Who is that so-called fan club? It refers to the Christians, churches, denominations, and other self-proclaimed followers of Jesus. Most people are aware of the longstanding history of injustices done to others in the name of Jesus, God, and Christianity: Religious persecution? Crusades? Inquisitions? Colonialism? Racism? Segregation? Red-lining? Misogyny? Homophobia? Bigotry?

To these questions of injustice, Christians may respond by saying that such wrongdoings are only a part of the past, or in the present, that they are due to "bad press," "fake news," or "sour grapes" on the part of their critics. Yet the questions persist — both inside and outside churches — and for good reason. It is important to remember that the bad behavior of Christians is not reflective of what Scripture has to say.

Let us consider an example: racism. Christians do not always like to talk about racism, since it is not explicitly mentioned in Scripture, or because it is an "ism," created by modern behavioral science, rather than by historic Christian ethicists. Many Christians claim not to be involved in racist attitudes or behaviors, even though racism continues to be one of the primary areas where Christians fail to show the kind of welcoming attitude that Jesus

5

showed to Nicodemus. Scripture says much about racial bias and discrimination, despite present-day efforts to ignore it.

Much of the book of Acts, for example, has to do with challenges due to the incorporation of a rapidly increasing number of non-Jewish (that is, Gentile) converts among the prevailing Jewish converts. In Acts 6, a group of service-oriented leaders called the deaconate was established—not because of an administrative oversight, but because of discriminatory practices against Hellenic (that is, Greek) Christians. Hebrew Christian widows were provided for in the daily distribution of food by the church, but the Hellenic Christian widows were neglected. Why? Scripture does not say, but it probably had to do with their different ethnicity or race, different language, or some other difference—an inequity that the church quickly corrected. Deacons were immediately appointed in order to promote the equitable apportionment of food and funds in the distribution of all that early Christians held in common (Acts 6:1-6, cf. 2:43-47).

Too often Christians and churches continue to be seen as instigators of racial, ethnic, and cultural insensitivity, or worse. Certainly these are not easily resolved problems, and religious attitudes represent only one factor that causes racism. But Christians would do well to heed Martin Luther King, Jr.'s, well-known critique of churches, when he said that the eleven o'clock hour on Sunday mornings is the most segregated hour in the United States. Again, racism is not an easily diagnosed and solved problem, but for Christians to minimize or ignore (that is, intentional ignorance) the effects of racism shows their neglect of Jesus' welcoming approach to people—all people.

Again, what of sinners? Did Jesus equally welcome them? Yes, he did. In fact, Jesus was condemned by his critics as being a friend of sinners (Matthew 11:16-19). Jesus identified sins, and exhorted people not to commit them. Sins include transgressions against biblical laws revealed by God, but sins have more to do with transgressing against God—of rejecting relationship with God or of reconciliation with God. Jesus did not cease to welcome sinners, and he did not take advantage of their faults to put them down.

All too often Christians fixate on actions that they regard as the sins of others and then use that perception of sinfulness as an excuse to exclude others. Christians and churches act judgmentally

6

and discriminatorily, acting self-righteously in focusing upon the "speck" in the eye of others, while ignoring the "plank" in their own eyes (Matthew 7:3-5). This is often the case regarding the issue of homosexuality. Let us consider this currently divisive issue: homosexuality.

What Scripture says and does not say about homosexuality has become increasingly debated among Christians and churches during the past century. To begin, there are not many biblical verses that deal with homosexual behavior. Moreover, the historical and literary context of these verses do not always provide the clear-cut conclusions that past Christians blithely maintained. In addition, Scripture does not address issues of homosexual orientation, homosexual marriage, or of transgender and intersex people. Given this background, some Christians—if not most—consider homosexual behavior a sin. However, they may treat these sins as being worse than other sins, even heterosexual sins, for example, biblical prohibitions about adultery, divorce, and remarriage.

Too often, Christians, churches, and Christian organizations act zealously against what they believe to be sexual sins, promoting church discipline and political laws against people who self-identify as LGBTIQ. However, they remain indifferent or accepting of those who commit heterosexual sins, including sexual harassment, assault, and rape. If Christians are consistent in their moral outrage and their exclusion of sexual sinners for the sake of moral purity, then perhaps they have reason to feel umbrage when they are criticized as being discriminatory, hateful, and oppressive of others. But if they exclude homosexuals from church and discriminate against them in society, while at the same time not acting similarly against those guilty of heterosexual immorality, then clearly they are as hypocritical as those Jesus denounced in Scripture for fulfilling parts, but not all, of God's teachings (see Matthew 23:23-24). Christians need to remember the first lesson that we learn from the story of Nicodemus: All are welcome!

Personal and Social Challenges

Christians want to maintain the moral purity of their lives and their churches, and Scripture supports this goal. The problem has to do with inconsistent, unfair, or discriminatory practices. Why is this so? There is a number of possible causes for these injustices, of course, personal and social. Typically, Christians have focused on personal causes: idolatry, pride, self-centeredness, and so on. However, they may not have focused sufficiently on social causes. In the United States, for example, citizens of the country have long been criticized for having a kind of "civil religion." Civil religion is a sociological concept about how people in the United States consider their nation to be indivisibly bound up with their understanding of God: God and country. More narrowly, they may consider their political party affiliation to be inextricably bound up with God: God and the Republican Party, or God and the Democratic Party. Although in theory, most Christians would say that God is neither a Republican nor a Democrat, in practice, they may not act that way. Close allegiance between God and a nation, or between God and a political party, results in the neglect of Scripture. People believe they are speaking words from Scripture, when they are really speaking words that come from a particular social group—an economic class, a racial or ethnic group, or even a political party. This culturally influenced view of religion leads Christians and churches into a kind of self-deception. They think that they are being morally pure, when in fact they discriminate against people or groups of people who are less powerful in defending themselves against violations of their moral and civil rights.

To be sure, Jesus was critical of certain people. Sometimes very critical! For example, Jesus criticized people's hypocrisy, and his greatest criticism was often against the hypocrisy of the religious and political leaders of Israel. In Matthew 23, Jesus condemned the scribes and Pharisees as hypocrites, blind guides, and whitewashed tombs, whose example should not be followed. In Scripture, Jesus repeatedly confronted the hypocrisy of Jewish leaders, not holding back because of their positions of authority and religious privilege.

Sometimes Christians appeal to biblical verses that seem to promote an almost blind obedience to those in positions of leadership, both church and government leadership. However, their hypocrisy is apparent to all—if not to themselves—when they advocate obedience only when their preferred church and political leaders are in power. They are often the quickest to condemn those same leadership positions, once their preferred church and political leaders are no longer in power. It is no wonder that hypocrisy is one of the most often mentioned reasons for why an increasing number of people neither like nor attend churches!

Final Comments

"What then should we do?" These are words that new converts asked John the Baptist, another follower of Jesus (Luke 3:10). To them, John gave very concrete advice: share; do not cheat; do not extort money; and be satisfied with your wages. Similar advice could be given at the end of this chapter on the topic of how Christians, like Jesus, should welcome others. Those within churches should focus upon becoming more welcoming, more hospitable, more loving—as they would want to be loved. Although it is good to abide by Jesus' teachings, we should do so even-handedly and not exclude or discriminate against any particular person or group of people, especially among those who are powerless, outcast, or suffering.

To everyone, I say welcome, just as Jesus welcomes you. Christianity should be known for welcoming all people, regardless of whether you are a sinner or not, and regardless of your race, ethnicity, sex, gender, sexual orientation, class, language, nationality, and religious background. This message of hospitality may seem too good to be true, and, in reality, it is not always the case among Christians and churches. But with Jesus, it is always true! Jesus welcomes everyone, just as he welcomed Nicodemus on that dark night.

Born Again? Anew? From Above?

I often tell the story about the conversation I had with a man while flying on a commercial airlines. The man sat beside me, and all I remember about him personally was that he was a dentist. He spoke to me first, noting that I was reading a book by C.S. Lewis, and asked, "Are you born again?" I was a theological graduate student at the time, and I do not know exactly why I responded the way that I did. Perhaps I was wary of what I considered to be overly narrow understandings of John 3:3, which says in the New Revised Standard Version of Scripture that, in order to see the kingdom of God (that is, be saved), one must be "born from above." In other translations, the verse sometimes says "born anew," and in the popular King James Version (and other translations) of Scripture, John 3:3 says that you must be "born again." I wondered if the man was testing me, requiring that I use an approved catchphrase in order to be accepted into his understanding of what it means to be Christian.

I responded by saying that I had drunk "living water." The man seemed somewhat confused, and asked the question again, "Are you born again?" This time, I responded somewhat differently by saying that I had eaten the "bread of life." By now, the man was disconcerted. So, I told him that I had used Jesus' analogies for salvation found in John 4 ("living water," v. 10) and John 6 ("bread of life," v. 35), rather than the birth analogy in John 3. Well, the man found my line of reasoning objectionable and insisted on talking about salvation as being "born again." I said I could agree with his terminology, if he accepted that Scripture contains many ways of talking about salvation.

At the end of the flight, we parted amicably. The man gave me his business card and told me that he would pray for me. He gave me the impression that his prayers would be more for my salvation, however, rather than for mutual understanding or for my well-being.

11

Salvation

For many people, talk of salvation from sin and death, and the promise of eternal life with God in heaven—by grace through faith—represents the pinnacle of the gospel message of Jesus. In the book of Mark, often thought to be the earliest of the four Gospels written about Jesus, the first chapter says:

> Jesus came to Galilee, proclaiming the good news of God, and saying, 'The time is fulfilled, and the kingdom of God has come near; repent, and believe in the good news'" (Mark 1:14-15).

What is this good news? The good news, or gospel, comes from the Greek word *euangelion* ("good news, good story"), from which we also derive the words evangel and evangelical. The terms good news and gospel may be used interchangeably. They may be used in general reference to Jesus' life and teachings, or to all of Scripture. They may also be used more specifically in reference to particular understandings of Scripture or subsequent church traditions, which place great emphasis upon God's provision of salvation through Jesus, and its proclamation.

For our purposes, I will talk about the good news of Jesus — the Christ (Gk., *christos*; Heb., *mashiah*—'anointed one') — in the context of John 3. Let's look at how John presents Jesus' understanding of salvation as it unfolded in his conversation with Nicodemus.

What Does It Mean to Be Born from Above, Anew, Again?

There are different interpretations of Jesus' conversation with Nicodemus, as one might expect, since it concerns such a crucial Christian teaching. Jesus said to Nicodemus, "Very truly, I tell you, no one can see the kingdom of God without being born from above" (John 3:3). Was Jesus speaking literally? Was he speaking symbolically? Was Jesus being ironic? Or, was John presenting multiple literary images for communicating about salvation?

Nicodemus seems confused by Jesus' words, not knowing precisely how to understand them. Of course, elsewhere in the book of John, misunderstanding the words of Jesus seems to occur repeatedly (e.g., 2:19-21; 4:10-15, 31-38; 11:11-13). So, Nicodemus responds literally, asking, "How can anyone be born after having grown old?" (John 3:4). Sometimes, when interpreting Scripture, a literal interpretation is the worst possible way to understand it! This statement seems shocking to some Christians, since they naively think that literal interpretations are the most factual, pious, and thus desirable. Despite this theory, in practice few Christians utilize a continuously literal approach to biblical interpretation. Otherwise, how would they interpret some of the Old Testament's wisdom literature, psalms, hymns, and poetry? For example, how would they interpret Isaiah 55:12:

> For you shall go out in joy, and be led pack in peace; the mountains and the hills before you shall burst into song, and the trees of the field shall clap their hands"?

Moreover, how would they interpret some of the New Testament's parables, hyperbolic preaching and teaching, and apocalyptic literature? Consider when Jesus said that if your eye "causes you to stumble, tear it out and throw it away." How often do you see self-blinded Christians (Matthew 18:9)?

Jesus continues to talk with Nicodemus about some complex theological ideas. It's clear that Nicodemus is no stranger to the study of religion in his own Jewish community. Their discourse involves some words and terms that might sound common to modern day Christians, but perplexing to non-Christians: water, spirit, flesh, Son of Man. The term "Son of Man" is a way that Jesus referred to himself, highlighting the fact that Jesus was human, and therefore understood the reality that humans like Nicodemus face. But in spite of the fact that Jesus is human, he constantly points Nicodemus towards spiritual things. Jesus said:

> The wind blows where it chooses, and you hear the sound of it, but you do not know where it comes from or where it goes. So, it is with everyone who is born of the Spirit, Jesus says (John 3:8).

Further on in their conversation Jesus starts talking about eternal life. He brings this up in the context of the story of Moses and the serpent in the wilderness, which comes from the book of Numbers in the Old Testament. In this story, Moses has just led the nation of Israel out of Egypt, where they had been kept as slaves. But once they escaped the land of Egypt they continued to struggle in the wilderness. One of these stories of struggle involves Moses raising a snake figurine on a stick in front of the people, as a means of healing them (this story is where we get the common logo for medicine, a snake wrapped around a pole). Although Christians don't necessarily know this story as well as Nicodemus did in his day, we can imagine that this story has a lot to do with healing and being rescued from trials and suffering. We are meant to have this association with healing when Jesus begins to talk about eternal life. Then we reach the climax of this passage—John 3:16:

> For God so loved the world that he gave his only Son, so that everyone who believes in him may not perish but may have eternal life.

For many years, it was common in so-called "red letter" editions of the Scripture to print these words as being uttered by Jesus himself. However, many scholars think that the verse contains the words of John, who narrated the story about Jesus and Nicodemus. Regardless of who spoke the words, many Christians have considered John 3:16 to represent the "gospel in a nutshell."

Words of Jesus

Regarding editions of the Bible that contain red letters for Jesus' purported words, in what sense do we know the literal words of Jesus? We know that the original New Testament was written in the *Koine* Greek language, but Jesus probably spoke Aramaic—the *common* language of the ancient Semitic world. Scholars infer this language usage because of occasional words spoken by Jesus that are recorded by Scripture in the Aramaic language, without translation into Greek. Of course, Jesus probably read and spoke Hebrew, which was the historic Jewish language. So, the words of Jesus were most likely translated first from Aramaic or Hebrew into Greek, and then from Greek into English (or other languages).

Moreover, the four Gospels about the life and teachings of Jesus were probably written, according to historical evidence, up to thirty to sixty years after the time of Jesus' public ministry. Scholars vary with regard to the degree of accuracy that Gospel writers reported the words of Jesus. Sometimes a distinction is made between "the very voice" (Lat., *ipsissima vox*) of Jesus, vis-à-vis, "the very words" (Lat., *ipsissima verba*). It is more likely that the Gospels contain mostly the "very voice" of Jesus, since the Gospels were written decades later, in a language different from the one used by Jesus. Some of Jesus' words may have been written word-for-word; however, Christians believe that God's Holy Spirit can convey meaning both ways. Consequently, the conversation between Jesus

14

and Nicodemus was probably a summary of key comments made, rather than the entirety of their word-for-word conversation.

This historical observation provides a helpful distinction, especially because of varying words attributed to Jesus in parallel Gospel accounts. Even if some of the very words of Jesus were precisely remembered by the Gospel writers, then their meaning would still face the challenge of translation into multiple languages — first into Greek, and then into English (or other modern languages). While we don't have the exact words of Jesus, we believe that the Scripture contains the essence of the words of Jesus — in other words, the "very voice" of God.

Generally, Christians have believed that Scripture is "inspired" by God, literally "God breathed" (2 Timothy 3:16-17), written by people moved by the Holy Spirit (2 Peter 1:20-21). As such, Scripture has been widely regarded as the primary religious authority for Christian beliefs, values, and practices. Its authority is a matter of faith, just as other affirmations about God, salvation, and virtuous living. More will be said about the nature and extent of Scripture's authority in a later chapter.

Heart of John 3:16

Most important is the content of John 3:16 — the heart of salvation. The verse talks about God's love, about God's sacrifice on behalf of humanity, and about eternal life available for those who believe. This salvation is not a matter of human action (or "works"). It occurs by grace, through faith; it is not a matter of earning salvation through meriting it by good works (Ephesians 2:8-9). The word grace essentially means a gift freely given, which enables saving faith. Salvation is a gift from God: it is initiated by divine grace, sustained by divine grace, and completed by divine grace. Yet, people are not passive in receiving salvation; they must decide to believe in Jesus and his teachings.

In general, Christians tend to lean towards one of two approaches to grace. The first is how grace works preveniently in the lives of people. Prevenient grace is defined as divine enablement or empowerment, which aids people in their decision to accept or reject God's gift of salvation. It is as if God holds out to people the gift of salvation in the palm of God's hand. God invites people to receive the gift, and God will help them to take it. However, God wants them to decide about whether they want anything to do with God and God's salvation.

Christians have differed throughout church history with regard to how they understand God's role for salvation. On the one hand, God graciously provides salvation; on the other hand, people are believed to share in responsibility for it. All Christians agree that it is only God, ultimately speaking, who can provide for people's salvation. Yet, Christians also agree that people have some responsibility for believing, and perhaps also for repenting, being baptized, and for receiving the gift of salvation. Differences in Christian belief between churches have to do with the degree to which people are believed to have responsibility for responding, especially for believing in Jesus for their salvation.

No Christians (or very few of them) believe that Christians are totally passive recipients of salvation, without any responsibility whatsoever in receiving God's gift of eternal life. Likewise, no Christians (or very few of them) believe that people must earn or merit their salvation, using only natural abilities. The overwhelming majority of Christians fall somewhere on the continuum between God's gift and people's action. Even people's faith is thought to be grace-aided, by means of prevenient or enabling grace. In other words, faith is just the first response in a chain of events that is made possible by grace for accepting God's gift of eternal life.

The second approach to grace puts more emphasis on the effectual, or irresistible, work of divine grace. This view emphasizes God's sovereignty and the compelling role of God, rather than upon the responsible decision-making role of people. From this perspective, we are to give all the glory to God, saying that we have done nothing. People still have faith, of course, but their faith is determined by God's election (or decree) that they will be saved. Their faith may be said to be compatible with God's election, but there is no condition on their part that warrants salvation. Using the analogy of God holding out to people the gift of salvation in the palm of God's hand, people indeed receive it because God directs their hands to do so. It is glorious that God saves such people, though they could not resist God's election of them. In theory — that is, theologically speaking — this view of divine grace is very appealing, since it places all the responsibility on God and no responsibility on people. After all, aren't people finite? Aren't they

16

sinfully depraved and incapable of doing anything that leads to salvation? Believers piously say: God did everything, I did nothing! In practice, however, Christians act as if their decisions make a difference, and that they are not wholly passive in relationship with God.

To be sure, there are mysteries involved with understanding the ways of God, including how God grants people eternal life. These theological distinctions are so important that they will repeatedly be discussed in this book, since people continually ask what God expects from them, just as they also ask what they may expect from God. In particular, the role of God for salvation and the role of people will be discussed in a later chapter.

Final Comments

The blessed hope that people have is the promise of eternal life — of salvation — through belief in Jesus Christ, of sharing in Jesus' life and in his resurrection. This salvation comes through no work, merit, or worthiness on our part. On the contrary, most people are acutely aware of their shortcomings, of their mistreatment of others, of their mistreatment of themselves — of their sin, of their separation from God, and of their need for healing.

John 3:16 tells us about the good news of salvation. We need to believe in Jesus and his provision for eternal life. All are welcome to believe! All are welcome to receive God's gift of salvation. All are welcome to participate in the greatest hope imaginable, by which God wants to bless us here and now as well as for eternity.

No Condemnation

When I began high school, I attended a Sunday school class at church for teenagers. A layperson named Mike volunteered to teach the class, even though his kids were in elementary school. On the first day of class, Mike said that we could ask any question. It did not matter what we asked! "Really?" I thought doubtfully.

Mike said that we could ask about contemporary issues as well as religious issues. We could ask about taboo topics that the church usually avoided, such as sex, alcohol, and war. At the time, the Vietnam War was at its peak, which included the draft of young men like some (and soon me) in the class. It was a scary time! Mike even said that we could talk about views opposed to church doctrine and policies. He would do his best to respond. There would be no condemnation about questions we asked. Mike said that, if Christians cannot ask questions, and if the church is not willing to discuss them, then what good is the church? What good is Christianity? Although Mike was not trained theologically, he dedicatedly studied Scripture. Mike said that he would come up with answers, even if the answers were not complete, or perhaps satisfactory, to us.

For me, the class was instructive, liberating, and satisfied a deep-felt need! This was true for others in the class as well. I was certainly in a formative stage in my life — intellectually, emotionally, and relationally as well as spiritually. Thus, I was drawn to the open, non-judgmental atmosphere of the Sunday school class. Members of the class asked questions: Lots of questions! Probing questions! Hard questions! To be honest, most of the questions were asked by the older guys and gals, especially those closer to the military draft age. But I looked forward to the class each week, since I knew that serious, real-life issues would be discussed.

Of course, not everyone in the class responded as favorably to the format as me. Some members did not want to ask hard questions. They found them threatening, possibly anti-Christian. Mike did not back down from class members. But when class members complained to their parents, who then complained to the

19

senior pastor, limits were imposed upon Mike and the class. In class, most protested, and we shared those protests with our parents! However, the leadership of the church—both the pastoral and lay leadership—were uncomfortable with the freedom Mike gave to teenagers in the class. But the boundaries put in place by the church leadership could not wholly prevent the class from being a life-changing and empowering experience in my life.

No Condemnation?

The verse following John 3:16 says:

Indeed, God did not send the Son into the world to condemn the world, but in order that the world might be saved through him" (*v. 17*).

Jesus' mission was not to bring condemnation upon people. His mission was to bring salvation to them, to reconcile people with God, to alleviate their guilt, to begin the healing process of restoring people in God's image, to provide a role model for how to live just and holy lives, and to overcome the temporal effects of death and of demonic forces.

Have you ever felt condemned or judged by someone? It's not a good feeling. People can be so insensitive and insulting. Words do hurt, despite clichés that say otherwise! They judge you for how you look, how you talk, or how smart (or dumb) you are. We're not perfect, obviously. But it feels like we're condemned more often than we're accepted or appreciated by others.

When people think of Jesus, condemnation should not be the first thing that comes to mind. Sadly, this is not always the case, not because of Jesus, but mostly because of how Christians and churches represent Jesus, in what they say and in what they do. To be sure, some theologies have arisen that depict Jesus as detached, unapproachable, judgmental, and damning. Perhaps more troublesome is that the actions of Christians and churches have produced more bad press, resentment, and outright hatred of Jesus, again not because of him, but because of how his followers have misrepresented Jesus and the gospel.

Justice and Judgment

Does this mean that God does not judge people, that there is no justice—now or in the future? No, that is not the case. In subsequent verses, John 3 reminds readers that judgment will come, and that condemnation will be fair. Most people want justice, even if it does not occur in this life. Who wants injustice to go unpunished?

Ultimately speaking, people's judgment and condemnation are due to *their* disbelief in God, *their* evil deeds, and the cover-up of *their* sinful responses to God (John 3:18-20). Keep in mind, God emphasizes justice as well as justification—equitable (that is, just) treatment in this life, as well as mercy (that is, justification) for eternal life.

Without going into a discussion of the many ways that people understand justice (e.g., retributive justice, restorative justice, and so on), both the Old and New Testaments talk about the importance of justice. Scripture makes it clear that justice matters to God as well as to how Christians ought to act justly as well as lovingly toward others. Although God cares about justice and judges people justly, the mission of Jesus was to provide for all people the opportunity for salvation, of forgiveness for sins and of reconciling them to God, and not to hinder people's redemption through condemnation.

Part of the problem in recognizing the non-condemnatory mission of Jesus has to do with how people, including Christians, conceive of Christianity. Too often people have a *depersonalized* view of Christian beliefs, which entails a proposition-based understanding of God. In addition, they should consider a more dynamic, *personalized* view of them, which entails a relationship-based understanding of God. Harold Englund talked about this distinction in his discussion of Christianity. From a depersonalized view of Christian beliefs, people think about (1) sin as the breaking of a law, (2) repentance as admission of the transgression, (3) faith as the acceptance of propositions (e.g., doctrinal statements), and (4) the Christian life as obedience to God's laws. While there is certainly biblical precedence for this view, it only partially represents Jesus and the gospel. From a personalized view of Christian beliefs, people think more about (1) sin as betrayal of a relationship, (2) repentance as confession, along with sorrow over the betrayal and the resolution to renew fellowship, (3) faith as trust in God, and (4) the Christian life as pleasing God, with whom you personally relate. There is also plenty of biblical precedence for this personalized view.

A depersonalized view of Christian beliefs is deficient, if separated from the personalized view. Likewise, a personalized view is deficient, if separated from the depersonalized view. It is not an "either/or" impasse; instead, it is a "both/and" solution. Both views help to provide a more complete understanding of God and Scripture.

People may become confused about Jesus and Christianity, or downright disgusted with them, not necessarily because of who Jesus and Christians are, but because of caricatures they have. It may be a problem of what I call "either/or" thinking, trying to understand the world, and perhaps God, with simple ways of sorting out what they think. To a certain extent, this is to be expected, since the world is too complex for understanding everything about it. We need useful categories for sorting out and labeling a constantly changing world. But either/or categorizations may prevent us from successful thinking, as well as successful living. We need to broaden our understanding. To be sure, this broadened approach to learning can be challenging and sometimes scary, but it is a matter of growing up. If we want to become adults, in our thinking as well as in our religious understanding, then we need to get beyond simplistic labeling. As Richard Foster said, the biblical exhortation to have *simple*, childlike faith does not mean being *simplistic* (see Matthew 18:3).

Guilt and Shame

Jesus talked about the guilt of sin, that is, culpability for sinful thoughts, words, and actions. If people are guilty of sin, then they need to repent. God graciously forgives people's sins, and indeed Jesus came to atone for their sins through his death and resurrection. Scripture speaks plainly: The state of sin is a terrible condition, in which one's conscience is pierced and sorrow and regret rightly occur. Thus, if one commits sin, then one can expect the tortuous feeling of guilt. Perhaps you've felt this to be true in your own life. It's not a good feeling, when you know you've done something wrong, or if you've mistreated someone. You may not be familiar or comfortable with the terminology of sin, but you probably know what it's like to feel guilty. It's the inescapable feeling that you have when you do something wrong!

Shame is not the same as guilt. They may occur simultaneously, but they are not the same. Shame has more to do with feelings about falling short of one's self-expectations or about how a person may be socially embarrassed. As such, people may feel ashamed about sins they committed. But the feeling of shame is different than the feeling of guilt, though the two may mistakenly be identified for the other.

There are many reasons people may feel ashamed, and sometimes it has to do with things over which they have no control. In society, people sometimes feel ashamed because they are poor, uneducated, or "live on the wrong side of the tracks." Others may feel ashamed because of their race, ethnicity, sex, gender affiliation, sexual orientation, linguistic ability, nationality, or religious affiliation. Sadly, people may confuse these experiences of shame as guilt, which is not correct. They feel bad, but not due to any fault of their own! Nonetheless, they may suffer, feeling as though they are deserving of condemnation, of some sort.

Do churches help people overcome the debilitating effects of shame? I wish it were the case. Christians can be just as snide, condemning, and exclusive as anyone can. Churches and the Christians in them may actually promote the effects of shame, simplistically (of self-interestedly) blaming people for their height (or shortness), for their poverty, for their racial identity, for their linguistic ability (or inability), for their age, or whatever, when in fact the people are guilty of nothing wrong.

Let us consider one example: poverty. There are biblical verses that you can find about the importance of hard work to be successful, and how laziness can lead to poverty (e.g., Proverbs 10:4; 14:23-24). But anyone with common sense knows that not all poverty is self-inflicted. People may suffer impoverishment due to the economic situation into which they are born, societal prejudices against their so-called class (including race or ethnicity), inherited diseases that people have, and tragic accidents or misfortunes over which they had no control. Such situations leave people impoverished financially and impoverished in other ways as well. It is noteworthy that, in Scripture, people sometimes questioned why certain people were poor, sick, or demon possessed. In other words, did they deserve it? However, Jesus did not ask such questions. He went about caring for the poor, healing the sick, and casting out demons, regardless of whether those afflicted were responsible or not for their particular impoverishment.

Today people should distinguish between guilt and shame, lest they unnecessarily suffer due to confusing the two. If people are guilty of sin, then they rightfully should feel bad. And they need to repent. However, if they suffer from shame, then people need to realize that the solution to their suffering is not repentance, especially repentance for no justifiable reason. Instead of repentance, they may need to change their attitudes, perhaps needing encouragement from a friend or a counselor. But they should be encouraged not to continue with an erroneous sense of guilt. Further, it is my hope that Christians and churches help people to escape this trap of misdiagnosed shame, rather than pouring salt in the wounds of shame that people suffer undeservedly.

Parent and Child Analogy

A common analogy that Jesus and others in Scripture used to talk about God's relationship with people is that of a parent and child — of a father and child, or of a mother and child. Jesus often talked about his heavenly Father, his *Abba*, which was an Aramaic term of filial intimacy. Using this analogy, we can better understand John's declaration that Jesus did not come to condemn. Scripture says that God sent Jesus to minister to people, to save them, and to lead them into abundant life, both now and for eternity. Like a parent, God does not want to condemn people — God's children. But sometimes parents discipline their children in order to enable them to grow into greater maturity, into what Scripture talks about as Christ-likeness.

When my children were young, there would be family chores for each of my children, which I posted on the kitchen refrigerator. I have three daughters, and if I caught one of them deliberately avoiding her chores, then there would be consequences. It would not be enough for my daughter to confess. Since I value a personalized understanding of Christian beliefs, admitting guilt alone is not enough, since people may be forced to confess when they are caught. Instead, I wanted my daughter to grieve over the personal betrayal of her transgression, and to promise not to avoid doing her chores again. As a parent, I could condemn my daughter, and punish her, and sometimes I did so with my daughters. I could also forgo my daughter's condemnation and punishment, and sometimes I did. Similarly, when it came to the salvation of humanity, God made the provision though Jesus' life, death, and resurrection so that mercy be given to people, who by faith would receive God's forgiveness.

Often parents are more understanding and accepting of their children than other people are accepting of them. The graciousness is analogous to how God relates with us — with we who are imperfect, with we who may not be good enough, compliant enough, straight enough or politically correct (or incorrect) enough.

Churches would do well to become more welcoming than excluding of people, especially those who are somehow different and, perhaps, condemned by society. As the family of God, churches may be hospitable to those who society ostracizes, often wishing that they would just disappear. Yet, Scripture reminds us that God loves everyone. Everyone. Everyone! God never gives up on us, and so why would churches give up on "the least of these" (Matthew 25:40).

Final Comments

As an attendee of Sunday school as a teenager, I greatly appreciated and benefited from an environment in which I did not feel judged or condemned because I had a question. It did not matter if my question was silly or due to ignorance. My teacher would consider my question, and try to respond to it empathetically as well as biblically and with common sense. My daughter Dana has been an especially dedicated advocate for the importance of empathy, and I think that she is quite right!

Jesus did not come to condemn people, but to save them. If we think about Jesus as a mean and vengeful person, no matter what the reason, then we have missed the point of his mission. Jesus came to save, to forgive, to embrace, and to give people another chance to receive all the blessings that God intends for us to have, both for life now and for eternity.

Part Two

"For God So Loved"

Yes, God Exists

When I was in college, I had a friend who wanted to debate with me about the existence of God. I wasn't sure about what to say. So, I asked if I could invite a guy I knew, named Dan, who worked with a campus ministry, to join the conversation. My friend agreed.

Dan came and disputed with my friend for over an hour about arguments for God's existence. In my opinion, the conversation was a fiasco. My friend was not convinced. Of course, I questioned whether he could ever have been convinced. Dan, the campus ministry guy, seemed self-satisfied, believing he had "defended the faith." But at what cost?

At one point in my early adult life, I doubted the existence of God. It wasn't a good feeling. In fact, it was a low point in both my spiritual and intellectual well-being. I remember sitting in my apartment, despairing over the futility of life. I felt weighted down, with few prospects for happiness. Ironically, it was a Jewish philosophy professor who helped the most in directing me to Christian literature that enabled me to decide key questions that I had about God.

Throughout my life, I have been in many discussions about the existence of God. To a greater extent, the discussions became more complex, in my opinion, when considering the challenges of postmodern as well as modern criticisms of historic Christian arguments for God's existence. Increasingly, I have come to conclusion that such arguments do not prove the existence (or non-existence) of God. They may be helpful ways for Christians to talk about their belief in God, but bottom line is that it is still a belief—not a rational or empirical inference.

I still talk about arguments for God's existence, and I will talk about them at length with people who are interested in the topic. However, I do not use these arguments to convince people that God exists. That is God's job, in my opinion! If people do not believe in God, then it probably has more to do with their ethical qualms or spiritual apathy, than it has to do with intellectual impediments.

Scripture does not seem all that concerned with arguments for the existence of God. Such arguments can be distilled from Scripture, but the convincing of people about God's existence seems to have more to do with the gracious initiative of God. More precisely, it has to do with the workings of God's Holy Spirit, rather than with the merits of Christian apologetics.

God Exists

Yes, I believe that God exists. I further believe that knowledge of God, that is, at least saving knowledge of God, does not occur because of human argumentation, but by God's gracious workings in the lives of people. Thus, I am interested in arguments for God's existence, but not for the sake of persuading someone to convert to Christianity. Knowledge of such arguments help me better to understand Scripture, and they help me to put into words my beliefs about God.

People who lived during biblical times were aware of arguments against God's existence. There were animists, polytheists, henotheists, monists, skeptics, and atheists. So, we ought not to think presumptuously that the authors of Scripture were unaware of or unconcerned about how people understood the existence of God.

Throughout history, arguments against God's existence have arisen. Most recently, atheistic proponents have challenged the logic or evidence for the existence of God, arguing for naturalistic dismissals of theism. For example, Ludwig Feuerbach argued that God is a sociological projection by people who feel inadequate. Karl Marx argued that God is a politico-economic projection by people who feel impoverished. Sigmund Freud argued that God is a psychoanalytic projection of people's subconscious selves. More recently, scientific argumentation has been used to denounce theism. Such atheistic denunciations depend on a belief that science will ultimately answer all questions that people have. However, science has not yet answered all of them! As such, a scientific worldview is as dependent upon belief as is a religious worldview.

As a worldview, science (or scientism) requires as much belief as does theism, though scientists use the langue of presuppositions, postulates, and axioms, rather than faith. Arguments for God's existence make as much sense rationally and empirically as does an atheistic worldview, if one seeks rational and empirical legitimation for one's argumentation. But Christians argue that their worldview relies upon more than rational and empirical argumentation. It also relies upon God graciously working in and through their lives. This working does not wholly remove theistic discussion from logic and evidence-based criteria, but affirmation of God's existence cannot be reduced to them.

Historic Arguments

There are several types of historic arguments for God's existence, and they have been considered foundational for Christian apologetics. *Apologetics* have to do with the defense of Christian beliefs, values, and practices, commonly by appealing to philosophy and the sciences for defending Christianity. Let us look at some of the historic arguments for the existence of God.

In the eleventh century, Anselm developed the *ontological argument*, that is, the argument for God's existence based upon rational argumentation. He argued that belief in God makes logical sense, and that it takes a greater leap of faith to maintain logically that God does not exist. After all, it makes sense to think that the idea of God — the greatest conceivable idea — exists in reality, and not just in the imagination.

In the fourteenth century, Thomas Aquinas advocated for *cosmological arguments*, that is, arguments based upon evidence in the empirical world. For example, Thomas argued that, in the world, there must be a first cause, or an unmoved mover, in order to explain physical phenomena. If something moves, after all, then something or someone must have moved it!

The *teleological argument* was Thomas's most prominent argument, which basically says that the world is too complex to have developed by chance. How could complex phenomena such as eyeballs, circulatory systems, and sexual reproduction develop by chance occurrences? Instead, there must have been a designer, namely, God, who created people, animals, and plants too intricate to be explained by random development. The teleological argument — sometimes called the argument for intelligent design — is probably the most common way that Christians argue for God's existence.

Charles Darwin's theory of evolution provided a scientific description of biological changes in species, but he did not speculate about the origin of life per se. Still, Darwin's theory remains one of the best known alternative theories for the biological development of life, supplanting the need for theorizing that God exists, who designed the complexities of people, animals, and plants.

Variations of the teleological argument for God's existence include almost any argument that requires a supernatural (or supranatural, preternatural) explanation. For example, appeals to religious experience, answers to prayer, miracles, and the pervasiveness of morality require that God undergird these widespread phenomena. Of course, most religions of the world claim similar supernatural occurrences. So again, the Christian affirmation of God's existence relies ultimately upon faith, rather than upon rational or factual proof.

I know Christians who cannot imagine how other people do not believe that God exists. They will say, for example, that they have felt God, had prayers answered, and perhaps experienced miracles. How could anyone thus deny God's existence? Although Christians may genuinely experience God in these ways, their experience is not the same as the experiences of other people. Christians cannot assume that their path to God will be the same as for others.

What about Scripture?

For some Christians, "Scripture says it. I believe it. That settles it." If Scripture talks about God's existence, then upon what other religious authority need one rely? However, the topic of religious authority is more complex, regardless of whether one knows about it or not. In the words of Scripture, the source of religious authority ultimately resides in God. But in this complex world, to what other authorities may people reliably appeal?

For many Christians, Scripture represents the rational and empirical foundation that legitimates all other claims to truth— religious and secular truth. But their claim to having certainty draws upon modernistic logic. That is, in the search for certitude, modernistic thinking appeals to rational and empirical evidence to undergird people's beliefs, values, and practices. It is comforting to appeal to rational and empirical arguments in defending Scripture, but it downplays reliance upon God and upon people's relationship with God's Spirit working in and through them. Nowadays Christians may feel intellectual solace in appealing to modernistic arguments for certifying their religious claims, for example, about the truth of Scripture. However, Christians have not convinced an increasingly secular world, which does not accept Scripture as being either a rationally or empirically reliable authority.

When Jesus lived, people were amazed that he spoke with authority. He spoke in contrast to religious leaders who regularly appealed to other authorities in proclamations that they made (e.g., Mark 1:22; Matthew 7:29). Jesus then gave authority to his disciples, for ministry and for leading the church (e.g., Mark 6:7; Matthew 10:1; Luke 9:1). Their authority in the Book of Acts was modified by time that the council in Jerusalem decided debates among the early Christians (Acts 15). Notably the council was overseen by James, an elder, rather than by the disciples (Acts 15:13-21).

For the next fifteen centuries, religious authority resided primarily in the leadership of the churches, both East and West. The leadership decided upon the content of the early creeds, and upon the canon of the New and Old Testaments. Thus, both chronologically and logically, the leadership of the churches, including the traditions that accumulated through their councils and magisterial decision-making, represented the primary religious authority of Christians. These groups of Christians gathered together Jewish writings (Hebrew Scriptures) and writings about Jesus (Christian Scriptures) and created a biblical canon, or standard compilation of sacred writings. This is the Bible as we know it today. Thereafter, canonical Scripture became increasingly authoritative, but the leadership of the churches determined its proper interpretation.

During the Protestant Reformation, Martin Luther argued that the leadership of the Catholic Church—the main western branch of Christianity—had become corrupt, and its traditions were no longer trustworthy. Instead, Luther appealed to Scripture as the sole religious authority for Christians. The slogan *sola Scriptura* (Lat., 'Scripture alone') became determinative in Continental Europe for Protestants' understanding of Christian beliefs, values, and practices.

Development of Religious Authority

Reformation also occurred in Britain with the establishment of the Church of England, or Anglican Church. Contrary to Luther and the Continental Reformation, Anglicans wanted to steer a *via media* (Lat., "middle way") between the traditions of Catholicism and the Protestant emphasis on Scripture alone. It seemed simplistic to appeal only to church authority or to Scripture. Instead, Anglicans affirmed the primacy of biblical authority along with the secondary, albeit genuine, religious authorities of church *tradition* and *reason*. Reason was considered a God-given gift by which people may discern between other competing religious authorities. Therefore, Scripture, tradition, and reason represented a "three-legged stool," so to speak, on which Christian decision-making best occurs.

During the Enlightenment, Pietist revivals broke out around Europe and the American Colonies. They emphasized the experiential dimension of conversion and the Christian life, which they believed was biblical, but which had been ignored. Revivalists like John Wesley emphasized the need to acknowledge *experience*, along with tradition and reason, as genuine religious authorities, which functioned interdependently with Scripture—the primary religious authority. Later Methodists referred to this fourfold understanding of religious authority as the "Wesleyan quadrilateral," including Scripture, tradition, reason, and experience. Nevertheless, Scripture was always the principal authority. Yet, Wesley recognized that tradition, reason, and experience impact our views of Scripture. This was good to know!

Acknowledgement of the role of experience in human epistemology has been crucial for contemporary dialogue among both Christians and non-Christians. To what degree is our knowledge influenced by our experience, that is, by our context, for example, by our particular socio-cultural situatedness? To what degree does our personal upbringing, or our ethical, political, and economic background influence what we claim as true? In addition, how does our experience influence our interpretation of Scripture? In interpreting Scripture, we also have to interpret ourselves, so to speak. A hermeneutical circle exists, which involves self-examination as well as the examination of biblical texts.

34

These questions about contextuality do not necessarily lead to relativism, but they do reveal that human claims to truth are subject to historical and critical scrutiny. It also forces Christians to remember that they live by faith, and not by the rational and empirical legitimization of their beliefs, values, and practices.

Nature of Faith

In Scripture, belief in God's existence is something thought to be aided by divine grace, as well as by human intellect. Christians ought not to be embarrassed by appealing to faith, or to mystery and paradox, with regard to their religious understanding. No other worldviews, including science (or scientism), have explained everything. They may appeal to presuppositions, postulates, or axioms, but those terms reveal their own faith commitments, even if they do not use that terminology. For example, science works on the presupposition that science will eventually explain everything—the world, people, spirituality, values, ethics, love, loyalty, and so on. As of now, however, science has not been able to explain all of the aforementioned phenomena by reducing them to biological, electro-chemical, or behavioral scientific explanations.

Belief in God is not, however, a "blind" leap of faith. This notion of a blind leap of faith is inaccurately associated with Danish theologian Søren Kierkegaard, who described faith as a "leap of faith"—as a passionate, existential trust in God, who is personal. But faith is not blind. Medieval Christians talked about faith as having, at least, three components: knowledge, assent, and trust. As such, Christians have *knowledge* about Jesus, and not about some other religious figure. They *assent* to knowledge about the life, death, and resurrection of Jesus, and they *entrust* their lives to the person of Jesus and to the gospel. Christians further believe that biblical claims about God as creator as well as savior are as reasonable as alternative worldview explanations. This belief does not prove the truth of the biblical worldview (or worldviews), but it does prove that Christian faith is a reasonable faith, and not a blind, unfounded, or simplistic faith.

Final Comments

I have often thought about my college friend who was willing to dialogue with me along with my campus ministry colleague about the existence of God. I do not know if my friend ever came to believe in God, but his willingness to dialogue gives me hope for him.

In my opinion, it is good to talk about God's existence and arguments used to talk about God. But it is not our responsibility to prove God's existence. I think that it is more God's responsibility than it is our responsibility. However, it is our responsibility to pursue greater understanding about God through all the resources that we have—Scripture, tradition, reason, and experience. Christians believe that God's Holy Spirit is always present and working in the lives of people—non-Christian as well as Christian. If God wants people to believe, then they need to be willing to do so. God graciously aids all who want to believe in God, both as existent and as their savior and lord.

God Is Love

When I was young, I heard several Christian speakers say that I should personalize verses of Scripture. Consider, for example, John 3:16. Instead of reading, "For God so loved the *world*," and so on, I should read, "For God so loved *me* that he gave his only Son, so that if *I* believe in him, then *I* will not perish, but will have eternal life." This personalization of God's love for me was enlightening as well as encouraging.

It is not insignificant that John 3:16 focuses on God's love. There are many ways that Scripture refers to God, and there are even more descriptions of God described by Christians throughout church history. But I think that focusing upon the love of God should be primary. Of course, it is important to think about God in other ways, for example, as sovereign, holy, righteous, just, eternal, and so on.

The book of 1 John speaks a great deal about God as love. Although 1 John shares similarities with the Gospel of John, it was probably written by someone else on behalf of those who affirmed the Johannine tradition. First John clearly says, "God is love" (1 John 4:8, 16). Elsewhere, Jesus summed up the 'greatest commandment' as involving love:

> One of the scribes came near and heard them disputing with one another, and seeing that he [Jesus] answered them well, he asked him, "Which commandment is the first of all?" Jesus answered, "The first is, 'Hear, O Israel: the Lord our God, the Lord is one; you shall love the Lord your God with all your heart, and with all your soul, and with all your mind, and with all your strength.' The second is this, 'You shall love your neighbour as yourself.' There is no other commandment greater than these" (Mark 12:28-31).

Furthermore, the apostle Paul talks about several Christian virtues: faith, hope, and love. Among these virtues, Paul says: "And now faith, hope, and love abide, these three; and the greatest of these is love" (1 Corinthians 13:13). Clearly love represents a decisive theme both for understanding God as well as the heart of Christianity.

Language about God

In talking about God, Christians have long realized that human language is inadequate for communicating the fullness of who God is. Since God is thought to transcend the world, including human understanding of the world, then ultimately speaking, the fullness of who God is will remain somewhat of a mystery. This does not mean that people's talk about God is nonsensical or meaningless. On the contrary, Christians believe that God has revealed much to us about who God is and about other religious matters, especially as contained in Scripture. Christians need to be humble, however, with regard to their specific claims about who God is.

As such, Christians think of language about God as being symbolic. The symbolic nature of God-talk does not mean that our language fails to communicate sufficient information about God, and it certainly does not mean it is nonsensical or meaningless. It simply means that God is above and beyond anything that we can imagine. If that is the case, how can our language not be, to some extent, symbolic?

Two ways that help me think about the symbolic nature of our God-talk has to do with distinguishing between analogical and metaphorical descriptions of God. On the one hand, analogical descriptions of God have to do with saying who God in like, sometimes known as *cataphatic theology*, using positive terminology for describing the divine. For example, in Scripture, God is variously described as being like a father or a king. Of course, the excellences of God being like a father or king is thought to transcend our human experience, both because of the finitude of our world and because of the effects of sin upon it. After all, people sometimes have bad fathers or bad kings (or rulers), who are negligent, abusive, or violent.

On the other hand, metaphorical descriptions of God have to do with saying who or what God is not like, sometimes known as *apophatic theology*, using terminology that is negative, or specifies our limits, for describing the divine. For example, in Scripture, God is described as being eternal, holy, infinite, sovereign, and unsearchable. These terms are familiar, and yet they are thought to transcend our full understanding of them. People's language as well as their knowledge of God are limited, again due to human finitude—finitude that is further impaired by various effects of sin, which effects all human understanding, including Christian descriptions of God.

The contextual nature of human understanding—involving global as well as national and regional understandings—further complicates the nature of claims that Christians make about who God is. We can only understand God through our own unique human lens. Often Christians believe that they have sufficient knowledge, including special revelation from God, in order to talk meaningfully about God. But it is a meaningfulness based upon faith, rather than certainty. As the apostle Paul says: "For now we see in a mirror, dimly…. Now I know only in part" (1 Corinthians 13:12). Our understanding of God will always be a little bit fuzzy, but it can still light up the room and shed light upon others.

Traditional Attributes of God

Christians talk about the attributes of God in many ways. There is no single way of doing so. Some talk about the communicable and incommunicable attributes of God; others about the immanent and transcendent attributes. In other words, how do we characterize God in a way that both speaks to God's nearness (immanence) and God's divineness (transcendence). These categorizations relate to our analogical and metaphorical variations of symbolic language for God. Some of the descriptions that we use to understand God are taken directly from Scripture, and others are thought to be implied in Scripture. Some of the descriptions draw from philosophical categories in order to talk about God. For example, some Christians have talked about the so-called omni's: omnipotence (all-powerful), omniscient (all-knowing), and omnipresent (all-present). Although these terms sound very impressive, they can misleading, both with regard to biblical descriptions of God and in terms of how people consequently live in relationship with God. They may reflect ancient Hellenistic views of God as much, or more, than they reflect Scripture.

Scripture describes many attributes of God that are just as impressive, and are more directly evident: benevolent, compassionate, constant, faithful, gentle, gracious, impartial, just, merciful, patient, persistent, spirit, wise, and so on. These latter attributes represent traditional or familiar ways of talking about

God, and they generally bring great encouragement to people who think about God, especially as they think about God in relationship to them. They often lead us back to the truth that is the title of this chapter: God is love.

Non-traditional Attributes of God

Although Christians tend to focus upon traditional attributes in description of God, a closer look at Scripture reveals some attributes that are generally neglected or repudiated, despite being biblical. I call these non-traditional attributes of God, since they describe God in possibly disconcerting ways. For example, God is described as angry, wrathful, and vengeful. In fact, there are more biblical references to the anger of God than to the anger of people. In the Old Testament, God orders the genocide of people, including men, women, children, and sometimes animals; God enables slavery; God is described as causing disaster, and possibly evil. If nothing else, God seems to change, or to renege on decisions, sometimes regretting (or repenting, depending upon the translation) decisions that God made. In the book of Job, God seems to boast to Satan — 'the accuser' — about Job, which resulted in a kind of bet or gamble with Satan, resulting in evil consequences for Job and his family.

How do Christians deal with these non-traditional attributes? To begin with, most Christians are not even aware of them. Often it is the case that it is not the people who are unfamiliar with Scripture that have trouble with its content; instead, it is the people who are familiar with it and with what Jewish scholar Phyllis Trible calls its 'texts of terror.' Sometimes Christians dismiss God's non-traditional attributes as mere anthropomorphisms. They claim that these negative attributes are merely examples of how humans have tacked their own baggage to understandings of God. However, this often involves picking and choosing which texts Christians want to take more literally, and which texts they want to take more anthropomorphically. Although it might make us feel better, this is not an honest way to read Scripture. Still other Christians appeal to the genre of such texts, or to their historical and literary contexts. But these interpretive acrobatics do not always grapple with the reality of Scripture as a whole.

But not all non-traditional attributes for God are negative. Some Christians might be surprised to know that Scripture offers a surprising number of descriptions about God that utilize female imagery, and also animal imagery to describe God. These are powerful metaphors and analogies that can help us learn about God in fresh, surprising ways. For example, in the Old Testament, Virginia Mollenkott notes that God is variously described as a homemaker, seamstress, mother, midwife, mistress, nursing, and having a womb. Elsewhere God is also described as a bear, eagle, and pelican. Again, what are we to make of this imagery? A common answer is that the majority of these references occurs in wisdom literature, psalms, and hymns, and as such use poetic license, rather than precisely describe God. Yet, the same can be true of the so-called traditional attributes of God, which are also found in wisdom literature, psalms, and hymns.

If nothing else, the non-traditional attributes of God should serve as a wakeup call to people, especially Christians, who are ignorant, at best, or misleading, at worst, in how they talk about God. Indeed, such people may rely—for their understanding of God—as much or more upon their own social, cultural, and religious background, than upon the evident teachings of Scripture. Humility, at least, should be Christians' response to the biblical characterization of God. What would an uncensored approach to God's attributes in the Bible look like? We need to ask this question, while recognizing the need for historical and critical interpretations of Scripture, rather than acquiescing simplistically to so-called traditional teachings about the attributes of God.

Stories of God

Scripture contains the story of God, or to be more precise, stories of God. It is worrisome to Christians to realize that there are competing stories, which recognizably come from Scripture. There are stories about God that pre-date Christianity, and today stories of God continue to arise, both within and outside of Christianity. Undoubtedly, we learn from other stories about God, stories that reflect international cultures, stories that reflect unfamiliar marginalization, oppression, and violence, and stories that reflect inspiring achievement, liberation, and restoration. Western Christians ought not to think only about how they may minister to others worldwide, but to think about how global Christians may minister to them.

Each person has his or her own unique story about God, whether it be from a Christian or non-Christian background, or whether it be from a spiritually positive background or from a spiritually negative (or, perhaps neutral) background. How people view God may be dependent upon factors not directly found in Scripture. For example, people may view God based upon their earthly father, which may have led to a very unloving, coercive, and unwanted image of God. People may also view God based upon bad experiences of Christians and churches they encountered. Who knows? But we ought not to let our background, our context, or our particular life situation to dominate wholly how we perceive God. There are so many more resources in the world to draw from, like deep wells about the knowledge of God.

Although Scripture is full of descriptions of God as all powerful, all knowing, and all present, I argue that its preeminent way of describing God is that of love. Whether you think of God as a loving parent, friend, or mentor, the trajectory of Scripture is to present God as one who wants to have loving fellowship with people—to forgive, to restore, to heal people from all that oppresses them. God is still sovereign; God is still holy; God is still all the other attributes that Scripture uses for God—the non-traditional as well as the traditional attributes. Scripture is not an exhaustive story-teller, but it is a sufficient story-teller, given the added belief that God's Holy Spirit continues to work in and through people in order to accomplish the gospel in their lives, individually and collectively.

Final Comments

I liked personalizing Scripture verses, and I recommend that readers try doing it for themselves. For example, it helps to say: "For God so loved *me*, that he gave his only Son *for me!*"

Because God is love, it is important that God give people freedom to choose—to accept or reject the gospel, to accept or reject God's love, to accept or reject eternal life. In a sense, God took a great risk giving people freedom to choose well, or to choose poorly. By analogy, it is like parents giving birth to children, knowing that as their babies grow older, they may love their

42

parents less, rather than more. Although human analogies break down, eventually, in describing God, they give us a hint of the love of God for people. More specifically, they give us a hint of the freedom that God gave for people to choose, the risk of not everyone becoming reconciled with God, and yet also the freedom for people to enjoy the benefits God intends for them to have, in this life as well as for eternal life.

Relationship of Father, Son, and Holy Spirit

Jesus had a very good relationship with God, his heavenly father. Scripture doesn't go into much detail with regard to paternal role models. Yet Jesus prayed to God long and often (Matthew 14:23; Luke 6:12), claimed to be "one" with his heavenly father (John 10:30), and referred to God in intimate terms. Why did Jesus call God "*Abba*" (Mark 14:36)? *Abba* is an Aramaic word that means father, but it conveys a more familiar relationship of "daddy" or "papa." Jesus' use of this name is significant for several reasons. First, it suggests that Jesus' primary language was Aramaic, the native language of the ancient Near East, rather than Greek or even Hebrew. Second, *Abba* suggests a more intimate relationship between God and a person than had ever been revealed before Jesus. Third, it suggests a relationship that was not just for the first century, but longer. Much longer.

Early Christians believed that Jesus was divine, and not merely human. If so, then what was his relationship to God the father? In Scripture, Jesus regularly refers to God as father, and he famously taught his disciples to pray to God as father. In what has become known as the Lord's Prayer, Jesus taught his disciples to pray as follows:

> Pray then in this way:
> Our Father in heaven, hallowed be your name. Your kingdom come. Your will be done, on earth as it is in heaven. Give us this day our daily bread. And forgive us our debts, as we also have forgiven our debtors. And do not bring us to the time of trial, but rescue us from the evil one (Matthew 6:9-13).

The words of the Lord's Prayer have varied over the centuries, been expanded, and modified. But the basic meaning remains. We are emboldened to pray to God as one would pray more intimately to a heavenly father.

Some contemporary Christians challenge the use of exclusively male language in reference to God. After all, does not God transcend male and female imagery, since all are created in the image of God, and are there not female images used for describing God in Scripture? Both of the aforementioned statements are true, and Christians would do well to remember both the benefits and liabilities of tying their conceptions of God too closely to maleness and femaleness, or to other contextual particularities of their view of God. But in theology, there is what is sometimes known as the 'scandal of particularity,' that is, we are limited — perhaps scandalously — with regard to the particularities of how God was revealed in Scripture. For example, Jesus lived as someone who was male, Jewish, and single. However, that does not mean he cannot be the savior and lord of those who are not male, Jewish, and single. Although it may remain somewhat scandalous, given the contextual nature of human knowledge, to think about God as father, that does not mean that such conceptions preclude a more universal gospel that applies to all people, at all times, and at all places.

One of the most radical ideas that Jesus communicated regularly to his followers is that we may approach God as more than a sovereign, all-powerful despot, far removed from us in heavenly majesty. We may approach God with one of the most intimate relationships imaginable, that is, the relationship between a parent and a child. We too may approach God as *Abba*!

Father, Son, and Holy Spirit

Early Christians thought of Jesus as divine — *Emmanuel*, Heb. "God with us" (Matthew 1:23, alluding to Isaiah 7:14). But they also believed that God the Father was divine. This was theologically problematic, since Christians — like Jews — were monotheistic, that is, they believed in only one God. What was the relationship between God, the father, and Jesus, God's son? Moreover, Jesus promised that God's Holy Spirit was to come after Jesus ascended to heaven, who would serve as God's representative on earth, along with serving as people's advocate and comforter. It was hard enough trying to explain God the father's relationship with God the son; Christians additionally had to explain their relationship with the Holy Spirit.

This relationship was a problem, not because of early Christian theorizing, but because of their strong commitment to the Scriptures that were passed along from the first century church. The early Christians didn't have a Bible, not in the way that we have the Bible today. They had collections of writings about Jesus, and collections of letters that Christians wrote to each other in the century following Jesus. When Christianity was made an official state religion in 313 by Emperor Constantine, the stage was set for Christians to meet in public and establish some consensus about what the church believed. This resulted not only in the canonization of Scripture that we know today as the Bible, but also a series of creeds that explain the faith that the Bible proclaims. Emperor Constantine called the first ecumenical (that is, all-church) council of Christians in 325, and a rough draft of the Nicene Creed was written and distributed throughout the Empire for feedback.

Based upon the Scriptures that Christians had available, it seemed that a great mystery surrounded the nature of God. Only one God existed, but how one conceived of that one God required a more complex explanation. According to the Scriptures, God the father was given divine names, ascribed divine attributes, performed works that only God could do, and was worshipped. Second, Jesus the son of God was given divine names, ascribed divine attributes, performed works that only God could do, and was worshipped. Third, the Holy Spirit was given divine names, ascribed divine attributes, performed works that only God could do, and was worshipped. Yet, the Father was not the Son; the Son was not the Holy Spirit; and the Holy Spirit was not the Father.

It should not surprise us that God transcends human understanding in more ways than one. With regard to how they thought about God, early Christians knew that they needed to develop some kind of summary statement, which could also answer critics who accused them of atheism (since they were not polytheists), tritheism, or worse.

Trinity

The Nicene Creed that eventually received ecumenical approval implied the doctrine of the trinity, though it was not until later formularies that formal references to the doctrine were established. The trinity is not so much a definition of who God is, as it is a statement about the limits of our understanding of God. Basically, the doctrine states that there is one God, who exists as three separate persons. As such, the trinity alludes to the mystery of God—a mystery demanded by Christians' fidelity to biblical sources. The doctrine did not result because of Greek philosophy or a concession to Roman critics, but because of the desire to be true to God's self-revelation in Scripture.

So-called heresies arose because of Christian attempts to provide more rationally plausible and socially acceptable conceptions of God. Some thought of God as one, who appeared with different faces (e.g., modalism). But this view did not do justice to biblical references to the differentiation between Father, Son, and Holy Spirit. For example, at Jesus' baptism, Jesus stands in the water for baptism; God speaks from heaven; and the Holy Spirit appears like a dove (Matthew 3:16; Luke 3:22). Another attempted solution was to identify the Holy Spirit as another reference to the Father, and Jesus was thought of as being who was less than God, or a supernatural creature like the angels (e.g., Arianism). Despite the logical appeal to these reductionist views of God, ancient Christians preferred to affirm mysteries associated with God's existence — as described in Scripture — rather than acquiesce to philosophical and societal expectations.

Whether you like it or not, the doctrine of the trinity represents one of the most unique characteristics of Christianity, distinguishing it from other monotheistic religions, such as Judaism and Islam. In order to explain the trinity, Christians sometimes appeal to analogies, some of which are quite humorous, in order to explain God. For example, God is compared with water, which can appear as a liquid (water), solid (ice), or gas (vapor); however, water, ice, and vapor cannot all occur at the same time (cf. modalism). Another analogy used is an egg, which simultaneously consists of a shell, yolk, and egg white; however, a shell, yolk, and egg are not all the same (cf. tritheism). Keep in mind that human analogies are finite, and they ultimately fall short in describing God. As such, one could say that the analogies are themselves heretical — at some point — since they do not communicate the fullness of who God is. Analogies can be helpful teaching tools to begin to explain the historic doctrine of the trinity, but no one should expect them to penetrate the mysteriousness of who God is, since ultimately God surpasses human understanding.

Development of the Trinity

Throughout church history, the trinity has been considered important for what is known as 'orthodoxy' (Gk., *orthos*, 'straight,

48

right,' and *doxa*, 'opinion, belief')—right opinion, or right belief. There is not Christian consensus about what orthodoxy consists of; generally, it is thought of as beliefs and values that reflect biblical teachings and early creedal formulations. However, neither Catholic, Orthodox, nor Protestant Christians agree on all interpretations of Scripture and upon which creeds (if any) to accept. Be that as it may, the trinity represents one of the more commonly agreed upon doctrines of Christianity.

The classic or traditional view of the trinity, at least, among western Christians, focuses upon the *immanent* nature of the trinity, that is, upon who God is. Sometimes focus is placed upon the *economic* trinity, that is, upon what God does, noting the different works or functions of each person of the trinity. Despite apparent differences, emphasis is placed upon the equality and mutuality of all three persons in the one God.

A more recent Christian view of the trinity focuses on the relational dynamics among the three persons within God. If God is one who eternally loves, then the love has always occurred between Father, Son, and Holy Spirit. God's love did not begin with the creation of humanity, but has always been a part of who God is. This view of the trinity is sometimes known as the *social* trinity, and it gives another insight into who God is. Although human conceptions fall short in fully understanding God, the social trinity helps us gain greater insight into the loving and relational nature of God.

Relational, Loving Nature of God

If nothing else, the doctrine of the trinity should remind us of a couple of important things about God. First, who God is ultimately transcends human knowledge, and yet we may have sufficient knowledge of God for salvation as well as for Christ-like living. Second, God is relational and loving, and that relationality and love extends to people for how they may be forgiven and reconciled with God, which further extends to how people may love others as they love themselves. Third, the trinity is practical. Yes, I argue that the trinity is practical because it helps us to realize the balance as well as the breadth of what Christianity includes.

For example, with regard to the practicality of the trinity, reflect for a moment about different ways that Christians think

49

about God, the Father: creator, providential caregiver, lawgiver, judge, defender of the poor, and champion against injustice. Next, think about different ways that Christians think about God, the Son: savior, lord, teacher, role model, healer, brother, and friend. Finally, think about different ways that Christians think about God, the Holy Spirit: advocate, comforter, empowerer, intercessor, fruit giver, gift giver, inspirer, and aider in discernment. Which of the previous works of God are most important? Christians would be horrified to think of one person of the trinity or one work of a member of the trinity to be more important than another. Yet, Christians sometimes emphasize the person and work of one member of the trinity over another; churches sometimes do the same. Thus, Christians and churches ought to be attentive to all persons of the trinity and to all works of the trinity with regard to how they not only understand God more fully, but for how God wants them to be and work in the world today.

Final Comments

When you think of God, especially God the Father, do you think of *Abba*? That is, do you think of God in the most intimate, positive, and supportive ways possible? There are many reasons for why we may not do this: current life problems, past personal misfortune, unhappy childhood, or dim prospects for the future? However, Jesus saw God as *Abba*, and when that happens for us, then we will be on the right path: for knowing God as Jesus did, for knowing Jesus as God's best representation for us, and for knowing the Holy Spirit, who is ultimately present with us now and wants to work graciously in prevenient ways in our lives.

Sometimes the doctrine of the trinity can seem confusing and foreboding. But it ought to be an aid for helping Christians and others to understand the personal nature of God, and of God's love for us. The trinity may also aid us in developing a broader, more appreciative understanding of all the ways that God works in our lives — past, present, and future.

What Apologetics Accomplish

In the ancient Christian church, the prospect of converting to Christianity was sometimes a matter of life and death. Christians died for their faith! Of course, the discrimination and persecution against Christians was not continuous. Violence was periodic. For example, as sensationalized in movies, Christians were not always being thrown to lions in the midst of grandiose coliseum massacres, though such martyrdoms did occur. For the most part, early converts were a minority group, usually neglected but often marginalized. Throughout world history, minorities are easy targets for bigotry and scapegoating, blaming (and persecuting) the poorest and most vulnerable for the problems of society.

For justifiable reasons, Christians did experience persecution, at least, from a civic perspective, when governments banned their religion. Overall, Christians considered themselves discriminated against unjustly. Few people came to their defense, and so increasingly, Christians had to defend themselves, sometimes bodily and other times ideologically. Ideologically, *apologetics* defend one's beliefs, values, and practices from caricatures or criticism. The word apologetics comes from the Greek word *apologia*, which means to explain or prove the acceptability of one's ideas. It does not mean to apologize or act ashamedly for them!

From time to time, all of us feel the need to defend ourselves—to defend our words or our actions. Perhaps we feel misunderstood, which leads to breakdowns in relationships with spouses, family members, and friends. Thus, we try to explain or clarify our words and actions so that we may become reconciled with them. Perhaps we feel unjustly attacked for who we are: where we were born, how we were born, and to whom we were born. Perhaps we feel attacked for our race, ethnicity, sex, age, class, ability, education, language, or nationality. We feel obligated to defend ourselves, even when we do not think there is anything that reasonably needs defending. Perhaps we feel attacked for our family or friends, for our social values or political views, or for our personal ethics or civic involvements.

Sometimes we defend ourselves when we know that we are wrong, or that we have done wrong. We probably should confess in such instances, and sometimes we do. Other times we do not, and defending ourselves becomes more difficult. Still, many of us do defend ourselves legally or morally, politically or religiously. Of course, when we have said or done something wrong—which we admit in our innermost selves is wrong—our self-defense may appear to others to be hypocritical or bullying or unscrupulous. Because we live in a fallen and sinful world, such tactics may succeed short-term. However, most of us wish that such tactics would not succeed, and that more justice would occur in the world, rather than less justice. Too often, the rich and privileged benefit from such injustices, rather than the poorest and neediest.

With regard to Christianity, there is an ongoing need to defend the faith, so to speak. Misunderstandings as well as critiques of Christianity persist. Sometimes, Christians can learn from their critics, since they ought to always be open to learning more about themselves and about how best to represent the gospel of Jesus Christ. Other times, Christians need to correct misunderstandings and feel the need to defend themselves from fallacious or unjust criticisms. Such is the task of apologetics.

What Do Apologetics Accomplish?

Early Christian apologetics commonly took two approaches: one was to engage with culture, and the other was to disengage from it. The majority approach was to talk about the gospel in general, and about Scripture in particular, utilizing examples and argumentation understandable to their contemporaries. For example, apologists such as Justin, Irenaeus, and Augustine appealed to Greek philosophy in order to communicate Christian beliefs, values, and practices. John 1:1 refers to Jesus as the "word," the *logos*, which is a Greek word that connotes the rational principle or standard that orders the universe. Christians spoke about Logos Christology by which they uplifted Jesus the one who gives meaning to all of life, both religious and secular. Philosophers such as Plato were thought to have foreshadowed or anticipated this understanding of the universe, and thus provided a philosophy that helped to conceptualize and communicate Christianity.

By contrast, apologists such as Tertullian argued that Christians should proclaim Scripture and church teachings without appealing to any other teaching or worldview with which to communicate the gospel. He famously asked, "What has Jerusalem to do with Athens, the Church with the Academy, the Christian with the heretic?" (*Prescription against Heretics*). In other words, integrating Christianity with anything or anyone outside of the faith runs the perilous risk of watering down or distorting Scripture. Thus, proclaim the gospel without any admixture of cultural ideas, philosophies, or influences that do not come from biblical Christianity.

Most Christians considered it beneficial to find culturally relevant ways to communicate the gospel, since they wanted others to understand their beliefs, values, and practices as well as to defend them. Broadly reflecting the premise that "all truth is God's truth," Christians argued that they ought to integrate the best ideas and philosophies, believing that they positively complement Christianity when utilized wisely, temperately, and justly.

Nowadays Christians increasingly acknowledge that all human knowledge — including their theologies, ministries, and apologetics — are culturally situated. In a sense, it is impossible for anyone not to be influenced by the particular place, time, and circumstances in which they live and speak. Similarly, when studying Scripture, interpreters take care to investigate the genre of a particular passage, along with its historical and literary context. Such studies help us to understand and apply biblical teachings.

In the 11th century, Anselm talked about Christian reflection as "faith seeking understanding" (*Proslogion*). Christians have faith in God, and in communicating that faith, they have drawn upon a vast array of ideas, philosophies, and other inspirations to articulate it to others. Sometimes their apologetical efforts were helpful; other times they were not helpful. Indeed, sometimes their apologetical efforts led to heresies, that is, ideas too dangerous for understanding and implementing the gospel.

Thus, apologetics is an ongoing task. It does not so much prove the truth of Christianity or Scripture, as much as it communicates the reasonableness of Christian faith, hope, and love.

At base, apologetists fulfill the dictate to always being prepared to give "an accounting for the hope that is in you" (1 Peter 3:15). The proof of Christianity requires the person and work of God's Holy Spirit in the lives of people, and not upon the excellences of rational and empirical legitimation of Christian claims. Salvation especially is due to the gracious workings of God and to the hope of future illumination, and not to the apologetical or evangelistic articulations of Christians. After all, Christians are saved by faith, and not by intellectual insight provided by rational argumentations or scientific evidences (2 Corinthians 5:7). Such articulations help Christians, though, to communicate more effectively and convincingly the logic of Jesus' gospel message.

A Brief History of Apologetics

One of the most prominent ways that Christians sought to defend Christianity to society at large was through arguments for God's existence. Anselm famously articulated an ontological argument for God's existence in the 12th century, appealing to rational argumentation. Thomas Aquinas summarized cosmological and teleological arguments for God's existence in the 14th century, appealing to empirical evidence for his argumentation. These arguments continue to be influential today, and they are discussed at length in an earlier chapter.

Over the centuries, counterarguments have been made against arguments for God's existence. Indeed, alternative arguments have been made, dismissing the need to believe in God due to philosophical, sociological, biological, psychological, and other objections. Because I think that people are saved by faith and not by human formulations, based upon reason and experience, I do not expect that anyone becomes a Christian by intellectual means. Some may find intellectual and apologetical formulations helpful in coming to faith. However, such formulations have more to do with articulating the reasonableness of Christianity, rather than proving its legitimacy rationally and empirically.

After the Protestant Reformation in the 16th century, Christians placed an increasing amount of apologetical energy in defending one church or denomination from other churches and denominations, rather than defending Christianity from its naysayers. In these endeavors, Christians appealed to Scripture alone (e.g., Reformers), reason alone (e.g., Deists), or experience alone (e.g., Liberal Christianity). Others appealed to combinations of Scripture, tradition, and reason (e.g., Anglicans), or to Scripture, tradition, reason, and experience (e.g., Methodists). These contextual approaches to religious authority served to defend particular churches and denominations; they also served to defend broader apologetical formulations.

The Enlightenment began with Rene Descartes in the 17th century, emphasizing the sufficiency of human abilities to discover undisputable truth. If religion contained truth, then modern people expected verification of religion by means of rational argumentation and empirical evidence. Revealed truth, for example, as traditionally found in Scripture, had secondary legitimacy, due to the priority placed on reason and experience. Over time, modern philosophers and scientists found historic Christianity less and less reliable. Scripture was subject to historical and critical interpretation, being viewed more as the result of human contrivance than of divine inspiration. During the 19th century, the truth and authority of Scripture especially came under attack.

As the modernistic thinking of the Enlightenment grew in society, philosophy, and religious studies, Christians felt increasingly delegitimized and marginalized as purveyors of truth. At the turn of the 20th century, various attempts arose to defend Christianity. Barth argued that Jesus Christ personally represents the true word of God, not Scripture. Scripture may indeed be fallible, but God uses it to encounter people in the existential reality of their lives and relationships. From Barth's perspective, Jesus personally confirmed the truth of the gospel, rather than the proposition-oriented efforts of Christian argumentation.

Fundamentalist Christians argued that the criteria for truth presented by modernistic thinking was correct, but that their conclusions were incorrect. Instead, fundamentalist Christians argued that Scripture is demonstrably inerrant, and that it contains no errors whatsoever, including matters of history and science. If Scripture differs from history and science, then the latter must defer to Scripture. From the perspective of fundamentalism, Christians need to battle for the truth of Scripture, presenting historical and scientific arguments verifying that errors are apparent rather than legitimate.

Other Christians argued that we increasingly live in a postmodern context in which the criteria for truth advocated by modern or Enlightenment people no longer persuade us. Humans are finite, and their claims to truth—even religious truth—are finite, relative to the particular time and place of making their truth claims. This does not make all truth relative; there are degrees of certainty. Claims about the physical world in which we live tend to be more verifiable by rational and scientific investigation; however, claims about beliefs, values, and ethics reflect more the situation in which such claims occur. For example, Christians may claim with certainty that they believe in a God who transcends finite limitations; they do so by faith. However, they must be humble in admitting that their affirmations—their propositional claims to truth—will always be subject to their own limited abilities to articulate God's transcendence, infinite nature, and so on. In addition, since Christians claim that all have sinned and fall short of God's glory, there is an added barrier to truth finding due to the myriad effects of sin in their lives and in the lives of others. Especially with regard to matters of eternal significance, God's Holy Spirit guarantees the truth of salvation, authentic Christian living, and eternal life.

Context, Deconstruction, Reconstruction, and Praxis

Christian beliefs, values, and practices do not seem to correspond precisely with any philosophy or anti-philosophy, or with any science, political ideology, or ethical system. There are points of contact, and discovering those points can be helpful to Christians in discerning what they affirm and then in communicating it to others. It is not an exact rational or empirical endeavor; however, and Christians need to realize their ongoing dependence upon God and God's living and active Spirit among us, lest we fall into the trap of thinking that God needs our defending. We need apologetics, of course, as long as people promote unbecoming caricatures of Christianity or as long as people unjustly attack core beliefs, values, and practices, and sometimes-attacking Christians with exclusion, discrimination, and violence.

In an increasingly postmodern world, Christians need to be aware of the contextual nature of their beliefs, values, and practices. They need to become more humble in recognizing the situatedness of themselves, their churches, and their denominations. Differences between Christians often have to do with the particularities of socio-cultural contexts, past and present. Contextualization does not necessarily relativize one's beliefs, values, and practices. However, it helps Christians to understand the historical background (context) that influenced who they are and how they should lovingly as well as contextually proclaim the gospel. This involves humility in not claiming dominion over all others, just as Jesus advocated a humble presentation of the gospel.

In evaluating one's context—personally and socially, spiritually and physically—new insights may occur. For example, people may discover that what they learned as children is less relevant now, needs modification, or needs jettisoning altogether. This process of deconstruction can be frightening, since it involves a frank reassessment of the past. University students may experience this deconstructive process when they leave home for school. They have to learn how to think for themselves, rather than rely upon the thinking of their parents, friends, pastors, or favorite role models in the arts, sports, and politics. Thinking for oneself can be frightening, and not all young people may do so with positive effects. This is why parents, in part, are concerned about their young adult children when they go off on their own. However, it is important for their personal as well as spiritual development.

From an apologetical perspective, it is important to deconstruct the arguments for Christianity that do not persuade you. Do not hold on to the rational and empirical legitimations that are unconvincing. Instead, affirm those people and ideas that you find persuasive. In particular, affirm those that help you reconstruct your understanding of yourself as well as of the world in which you live. After all, from a Christian perspective, God's Holy Spirit is believed to be with you all the time—guiding you, enabling your decision making, and empowering you to find truth about yourself and your relationship with God and others.

After recognizing the contextual nature of one's life, beliefs, values, and practices, there definitely needs to be a reconstruction that occurs. Deconstruction ultimately contributes to this process of reconstruction, since one needs to develop a more realistic understanding of what influenced you in the past, and of what you want to influence you in the future. From a Christian perspective, consideration of both theory (*theoria*) and practice (*praxis*) is necessary. Praxis is a word increasingly used by Christians to say that determining their beliefs alone is insufficient; do not focus only on what to believe but also on what to do and to create (*poiesis*). Praxis involves more than practical applications of one's beliefs. It involves a holistic integration of faith, hope, and love, emphasizing hope and love that manifest in holistic ways. Defending Christianity in an apologetical way involves showing demonstrably that religion makes a difference. It is not all theory; it tangibly affects people's lives physically as well as spiritually, socially as well as individually. Christian faith, hope, and love saves souls; they also tend to people's physical needs. Christianity advocates for justice as well as for righteousness, cares for the poor as well as cares for the poor in spirit, and champions temporal peace as well as eternal peace that surpasses all understanding.

Final Thoughts

We need apologetics, since Christianity has been repeatedly misunderstood and mistreated, through verbal and physical abuse. The need continues today. Apologetics may not prove the truth of Christian beliefs, values, and practices. However, they help to show the reasonableness of their affirmations and the praxis of their lovingkindness.

Ultimately, God guarantees the truth of historic Christianity, rather than our apologetical efforts. Still, our apologetical efforts help Christians to explain their beliefs, values, and practices in ways that are understandable. They may also serve as the means by which God's Holy Spirit works in the lives of people to convince them of their sinful separation from God, and of the need for them to convert to the gospel of Jesus Christ and to live in accordance with his teachings.

Part Three

"The World"

Created and Evolved

I grew up camping with my family every summer in Yosemite National Park, and I loved everything about it, especially Yosemite's dramatic geological formations carved by glaciers over millions of years. But the stories I learned about geological and biological evolution from school, science, and even national parks did not match what I learned in church. Although the church I attended as a child did not have an official position on creation and evolution, the default was a simplistic appeal to a creationist affirmation of a young earth that had not evolved. When questions were asked of family and church friends, too often I received partial, wishy-washy, or uncritical statements thought to be pious, but were personally and spiritually as well as scientifically detrimental.

It amazes me how some Christians live in continual denial of science. They love science when it makes them money, helps them predict weather, or provides pleasure for them for entertainment or health. But they hate science and scientists when they talk about the origin of the universe (which offends their simplistic interpretations of the creation story), biological evolution (which offends their simplistic understanding of what it means to be human), or global climate change (even though they plan their work or vacation plans based upon meteorological science). Unintentionally, such simplistic views of science leave their most vulnerable loved ones even more vulnerable: children. When Christian children go to school, too often they are unprepared — intellectually as well as emotionally — to deal with the incongruities they are taught about science and religion. Some parents deal with the incongruity by contributing to their denial of the topic, removing their children from public schools. In the end, children are left vulnerable if they do not receive a fact-based education about scientific matters.

As I have grown older, I have become increasingly convinced by the saying: All truth is God's truth. Scripture talks to us primarily about spiritual and religious matters, whereas science talks to us about empirical and behavioral truths that can be measured quantitatively, qualitatively, and in other ways. Similarly, as western science developed during the Middle Ages, Christians talked about two books: Book of Nature, and Book of Scripture. These are books in a metaphoric and a literal sense. We can "read" about God's awesomeness in marvels of the created world, just as we can read about God in the Scripture. Although overlap occurs between the two books, the range of their understanding, competence, and authority differed. Christians sometimes feel like they have to choose between the two: the book of nature and the book of Scripture. But in reality both of these books have a lot to tell us about God and creation, and we can read them both together.

Book of Genesis

The first book of Scripture is Genesis, which means "origin," and it contains stories about the origin of the world, people, sin, and more. How are we to interpret these stories — these accounts of how things came to be before there were people to observe them? Throughout church history, there have been many interpretations. Some think the universe and earth are young, not more than 6,000-10,000 years old, based upon a literal interpretation of dates in Genesis. Other Christians think that God created all things, but that there are explanations for why the earth is millions and billions of years old. For example, a recreation or 'gap' in time may have occurred after Genesis 1:1, or biblical references to six days of creation may have meant an era or epoch of time, which lasted much longer than a 24-hour day. Still others think that the creation stories were literary productions intended to contrast Jewish beliefs with those of other Near Eastern creation stories, which were prevalent in the ancient world. As such, they contain important theological teachings, but not scientific descriptions of the world.

In the early church, Christian leaders such as Origen and Augustine did not think that the literal interpretation of the creation stories is the best interpretation of Genesis. Too many chronological and logical incongruities occur, and so they argued that a symbolic or allegorical interpretation was better, since such interpretations anticipated (or prophesied) more important Christian teachings about salvation. Some Christians think that people have only begun to challenge a literal interpretation of the Bible in modern times, following the rise of modern science and Darwin's theory of evolution in the 19th century. This is simply not the case, as the writings of Origen and Augustine can attest. But, since the rise of science and evolution, quite a few Christians have staked the truth of their interpretation of all Scripture upon a literalistic interpretation of Genesis, establishing a 'creation science' in order to legitimize some of the incongruities between their claims and those of peer-reviewed scientists.

Creatio ex Nihilo

Regardless of one's interpretation of Genesis, Christians have believed that God — ultimately speaking — created the universe and people. In the language of the early church, God created *ex nihilo* (Lat., 'from nothing'). This claim contrasted Christianity with alternative views of creation that understood God as an artistic shaper of pre-existing reality, who was a finite rather than infinite God. Christians agreed that God created all things, which had profound implications for humanity.

Let us consider some of the implications of creation *ex nihilo*. First, Genesis says that creation was "good." This goodness includes the physical world in which we live. In contrast to Judeo-Christian religions, which only emphasized the goodness of spiritual realities, Christianity affirmed the goodness of the world, of our physical bodies, and of how one treated the physical world. Second, God created the world with purpose or intentionality. It was not a random world, in which nothing is of ultimate importance. Rather, there is purpose both for the world and for the people in it, which encompasses their physical existence.

Regrettably, Christians have not always valued the physical dimension of the world in which they live as much as the spiritual dimension. As a result, Christians have been criticized as being so heavenly minded that they are of no earthly good. This omission is especially regrettable since, in Genesis 1:28, people are instructed by God to have "dominion" over the world, along with other instructions. Yet, over the centuries, it seems that people — including, and sometimes primarily, Christians — have understood their dominion over the world as permission to exploit it, rather than to care for it. Some contemporary Christians advocate for what they describe as 'creation care,' or Christian environmentalism, which honors God's instruction for dominion-having, rather than for self-serving exploitation of God's good creation.

Religion and Science

Although one may affirm that all truth is God's truth, how should religion and science relate with one another? Ian Barbour talks about four types of relationship: conflict, independence, dialogue, and integration. Conflict seems non-productive, both for science and religion. Independence of science and religion just seems to leave both in a perpetual state of denial. Dialogue certainly needs to occur, even though mutually satisfactory communication has experienced fits and starts. Integration may seem ideal, but such hopes lie far in the future. In the meantime, dialogue seems the most realistic, even though Christians historically have been inconsistent in their dialogue with scientists. Even if Christians claim that scientists have been equally inconsistent (or worse), it is incumbent upon Christians to seek greater understanding, scientifically as well as theologically, if their presentation of the gospel is to have integrity, given the breadth of their worldview claims.

Throughout church history, Christians have vacillated in their understanding of science and religion. Some have emphasized a supernatural worldview (e.g., supernaturalism, occasionalism) in which the events of nature and human decision-making are predetermined by God, before the world was created. This point of view is compelling for a number of reasons, not the least of which attributes all power and events to the sovereignty of God. Despite a pious regard for God's sovereignty, most Christians do not live this way. Nor have most of their theologies advocated it. As an example, when was the last time you heard a Christian say that the grocery store ran out of bananas because God predetermined that it would be so? Or, on a more serious note, how many Christians firmly believe that God predetermined a person would have cancer, or commit suicide?

Instead, most have affirmed a Christian naturalism — consciously or unconsciously — that affirms God as the primary cause of natural and human phenomena, but which allows for secondary causation. As such, nature and people have intrinsic power that allows them, by God's grace, a measure of independence. For example, nature functions according to physical laws, which can be studied and understood apart from supernatural causation. Nature evolves because of random events that occur, due to physical, biological, and behavioral dynamics. So, we benefit from scientific studies of nature. When apparent conflicts arise between science and religion (e.g., flat earth, earth as the center of the universe), then Christians may need to adjust both their understandings of science and religion. This includes their interpretations of Scripture. If indeed all truth is God's truth, then premodern and prescientific interpretations of Scripture ought not to continue, just because they represent longstanding traditions of interpretation.

With regard to people, Christians have mostly believed that everyone has a measure of independence or freedom. Otherwise, how could God hold people accountable for sin, if they have no personal responsibility for their decision-making? Of course, people do not have absolute freedom. There exist many limits to freedom; people are finite, live in various different contexts, personally and socially, and are also thought to struggle against the powers of sin and evil. Be that as it may, Christians mostly believe that they (and all people) have a measure of freedom, but that they still need God's gracious assistance for their salvation.

Just as there are elements of randomness in nature, there are elements of randomness in the events of life. Not every event reveals a meticulous divine plan; instead, circumstances occur due to random events, bad luck, or unwise decisions—by one's own decisions, or by the decisions of others. God's plans may be thought to occur in more general terms, providing a context in which secondary causes apply, rather than believe that God meticulously causing everything. Thus, the scientific and behavioral scientific study of humanity may aid people as well as Christians in how they understand and respond to life circumstances.

Christianity and Evolution

Contrary to popular belief, Christians can benefit from the theory of evolution, along with its ongoing research into biological and other physical realities. Christianity and evolution are not mutually exclusive, at least, not to the degree that evolution is viewed in its micro-manifestations as an investigative scientific tool.

When evolution becomes an explanation of all things, then it ceases to be a scientific theory similar to other scientific theories (e.g., gravity, relativity). Instead, it becomes a worldview, an 'ism,' which intends to serve as a macro-explanation for all of life. Such an intention requires as much belief as any other worldview, and becomes less persuasive both to religion and science.

In the meantime, Christians benefit greatly from the advances in science that come from the theory of evolution. They learn important lessons about human physiology, past biological developments, and the prospect of future developments that may help them for more than medical reasons. Rather than waste time in conflict with science, Christians would do well to dialogue with it and learn how their faith, including their understanding of Scripture and the Christian life, may benefit from scientific and behavioral scientific research.

Benefits from science already occur, which are implemented both by Christians and churches, for example, applying psychological and sociological insights. However, they often fail to attribute these benefits to science. Instead they tack on biblical verses to behavioral scientific insights, claiming disingenuously that Scripture foretold them.

It may be that Christians need to begin their historical understanding of Judaism and Christianity with Abraham, more than with Genesis 1-11. Theological lessons may be learned from the creation stories, but their benefit comes more from what they teach about God, humanity, and sin, than from what they teach about geology and biology. But such a prospect should not be considered more daunting than those who lived during the fifteenth and sixteenth centuries, when Christians needed to come to grips scientifically with evidence that the world is neither flat nor the center of the universe.

Final Comments

As a Christian, I find the theory of evolution liberating, since I do not view religion and science in conflict. At times, we may need to enhance our understanding of Scripture with empirical data, which improves our overall worldview as Christians, scientifically as well as religiously. In practice, we do this all the time in medicine, agriculture, and other areas of daily life. How much have we benefited medically from evolutionary studies that led to advances in bacterial antibiotic resistance and vaccines? How much have we benefited agriculturally from evolutionary principles in crop breeding, domestication of animals, and pest resistance?

Too many people, especially children, are vulnerable to confusion and unnecessary struggle, due to Christians' unwillingness to acknowledge that all truth is God's truth. After all, it is not up to Christians to defend God; God does not need defending. Instead, God wants Christians to proclaim the gospel, as found in Scripture, even though Scripture does not address every conceivable question or concern that people have about the nature of the universe.

People and the Image of God

When reading definitions about what it means to be human, often empirical and biological information is given: People represent bipedal primate mammals (*Homo sapiens*), with advanced brain development, and capacity for reasoning and speech, which contrasts with other animals. While biologically correct, most people would say that being human involves more. Much more! But what more does it involve? How do we communicate people's facility in culture, art, music, sports, science, and technology? How do we communicate people's values, for example, love: love for self? love for children? love for friends, community, or nation? There are many intangible aspects of what it means to be human — aspects which most people would not want to deny, or reduce to biological and/or electrochemical functions — and yet difficult to prove or explain empirically by means of science.

Scripture talks about people as being created in the image of God, and this affirmation profoundly influenced how both Jews and Christians understand what it means to be human. Genesis states that God created people, and that they were uniquely created in God's image. Genesis 1:27 says:

So God created humankind in his image, in the image of God he created them; male and female he created them.

Scripture does not say precisely what it means to be created in God's image. Many theories, as one may imagine, have arisen. Yet the consensus has been that people are different, and that phenomenal observation and scientific research alone are inadequate to encapsulate the whole of what it means to be human.

There are competing explanations for what it means to be human, all of which rely on some ideological assumption or leap of faith: Hinduism? Judaism? Buddhism? Christianity? Islam? Scientism? Evolution? Humanism? Christians argue that explanations for what it means to be human will all fall short if they exclude a spiritual dimension, or a dimension of relating to the divine, that is, God. This is a faith statement, of course, but

Christians say that it is a reasonable affirmation given all that we know about people — past and present.

Imago Dei

The image of God (Lat., *imago Dei*) encapsulates for Christians the uniqueness of what it means to be human. Despite the prominence that Christians give to the image of God in people, there has not been consensus with regard to what it means. In Genesis, much is said about what it means to be human with regard to what they look like, what they are do, and how they have multiple relationships, including a relationship with God. But neither Genesis nor other passages in Scripture define precisely what it means to be made in God's image.

Throughout church history, various attempts have been made to understand the image of God. Some have thought that there is a *substantive* explanation. For example, people are thought to reflect God's image because of their rationality, spirituality, or some other substantive aspect of who they are, such as a soul. Others have thought that there is *functional* explanation. For example, God commanded people to be moral, and they reflect the image of God to the degree that they act morally; or God commanded people to have dominion over the world, and they reflect the image of God to the degree that they have dominion. Still others have thought that there is a *relational* explanation. For example, people reflect God's image to the degree that they are in a right relationship with God, themselves, or others. In my opinion, each point of view contributes to the whole of what it means to be human, without exhausting all the dimensions of it, since there may be new things that we still need to learn about the fullness of God's image.

Whatever it means to reflect God's image, it probably involves more than what people are individually. Since Scripture says that both men and women were created in the image of God, then no single individual necessarily reflects all of it. Broadly speaking, Christians would argue that some kind of spirituality and relationality, including people's relationship with God, is inextricably bound up in what it means to be human — truly human, as Scripture describes people as being in God's image. People may be studied and helped in many ways, but the fullness of who people are cannot be achieved until their spirituality and relationship with God are acknowledged, prioritized, and made right.

What Is the Soul?

At times people think about being (or having) a soul as somehow making them unique, even spiritually unique. Scripture certainly makes a number of references to people's souls. But the concept of a soul was not unique to Jews and Christians. References to it appear throughout the ancient Near East, among religious as well as non-religious people. As a result, Christians are likely confused about there being a consensus, or not, regarding what should be believed about the nature of a soul.

For Christians, part of the problem is that Scripture gives no determinative statement about souls. Sometimes people are described as having a body and soul (e.g., Matthew 10:28), which suggests a dualistic or *dichotomous* view of people. Other times people are described as having a body, soul, and spirit (e.g., 1 Thessalonians 5:23), which suggests a *trichotomous* view of people. Contemporary debates have continued among Christians with regard to whether people *have* a soul, which is a spiritual reality, or whether they *are* spirited bodies, which do not have discreet souls per se (e.g., nonreductive physicalism).

Are the biblical authors making ontological pronouncements, specifying that categorical references to people be made exclusively to having a body and soul, or to having a body, soul, and spirit? I do not think so. I think that Scripture contains a variety references to what it means to be human, without articulating a single right way to look at it. For example, in describing the greatest commandment, Jesus told people to love God with their whole heart, soul, mind, and strength (Mark 12:30), but does this reference represent a tetrachotomous, or four-part view of people? Scripture is filled with many images to communicate the need to attend to spiritual matters, and not necessarily to hard-and-fast descriptions of what it means to be human. Yes, it is correct to refer to people as souls, with spiritual identities. But biblical references to a person's soul have more to do with talking generally about an individual 'self,' rather than about a philosophical framework for the self, distinguishable from one's body, spirit, heart, mind, or strength.

If the soul is a general, descriptive reference to oneself, then people may be thought of as a complex unity, more than a conglomeration of individual parts. Christians today may debate between different theories about people: dualistic and monistic views, reductive and non-reductive views, and so on. However, thinking about the complex unity of people helps us to remember, first, that people are individuals and that individuality is an inescapably important aspect about who they are, and second, that there may be no end to learning about the complexity of who people are, and the variety of relationships they have. I suspect that, the longer we live, the more we will learn about ourselves from science and the behavioral sciences as well as from Scripture.

Individual and Social

Too often people think about themselves as individuals — as rugged individuals, self-made people, islands in the sea. The individualism of western society has reinforced this understanding of people, distancing themselves, including Christians, from one another. Yet in the history of the world, as well as church history, individualism is relatively new; that is, the notion that people are self-reliant and that they should be free to act, regardless of collective or social relations. Scripture as well as most of church history gives a different perspective.

Although humanity is made up of individuals, they are inextricably bound up with one another. In the Old Testament, God dealt with Israel as a nation, as well as with individuals in it. In the New Testament, God dealt with the church as a whole, as well as with individuals in it. When people today, especially Christians, think that individual rights trump social rights, and that individual well-being has nothing to do with social well-being, then a great loss has occurred. That loss may even include a loss of what is meant by the image of God in Scripture. There is no reason to think that God's image should be understood individualistically. Thus, Christians should be as concerned about the well-being of their social relations as they are concerned with their own well-being. This social understanding of what it means to be human coincides with Jesus' command to love our neighbor as ourselves. Our neighbor is not limited to loving people individually; it includes

72

love toward groups of people, and not just toward our immediate family or friends, tribe or nation.

Although there is no necessary correlation between the trinity and image of God in which people were created, the relationship between father, son, and Holy Spirit should remind us that relationality is not incidental to what it means to be human. If Christians want to love their neighbors as themselves, then they should not only be concerned about the spiritual, physical, and moral well-being of individuals they meet. They should also be concerned about the spiritual, physical, and moral well-being of people groups — locally, nationally, and around the world.

Male and Female

Genesis 1:27 says that both men and women were created in God's image, suggesting equality in the quality of who they are. Throughout history, however, patriarchy has dominated male and female relationships, and Scripture has been thought to corroborate a hierarchical relationship in which men always have authority over women. As such, patriarchy has to do with structuring society along male lineage, having men govern women, and prioritizing the interests of men over those of women and children. Contemporary advocates of patriarchy sometimes prefer to use the term complementarian, since it doesn't have the same bad connotation that patriarchy does. Such advocates argue that the differing roles and functions played by men and women are thought to complement one another, rather than diminish them. But they maintain this view while affirming that men are the natural leaders and heads of society.

Sometimes patriarchy is thought to be determined by God's hierarchical order of creation, and thus to oppose patriarchy is to oppose God. Sometimes patriarchy is thought to be a result of the fall of humanity into sin, and thus the subordination of women to men is a just punishment. Still others argue that hierarchy exists within the trinity, and so women ought to submit to a paternalistic-oriented revelation of God's trinitarian nature.

Although hints of egalitarianism have arisen throughout church history, only recently have women been given equal opportunities by Christians within marriage, in society, and even church leadership. There is no one single argument that is used;

however, here are some biblical arguments used for liberating society from patriarchy. First, there are examples of women leaders in Scripture (e.g., Deborah, Miriam, Mary Magdalene, Priscilla). Second, patriarchalism is not consistently present in Scripture. Notably, Paul's writings are inconsistent when it comes to gender roles; sometimes he talks about how women ought to be silent in church, and other times he talks about how they ought to speak publicly in church (1 Cor. 11:4-5, 16, vis-à-vis, 1 Cor. 14:33b-35). Third, the Holy Spirit equally gifted males and females, and denial of the exercise of these gifts hinders God's work (Acts 2:17; 1 Cor. 12:4-11). Fourth, principles of equity are promoted, for example, Galatians 3:28: "There is no longer Jew or Greek, there is no longer slave or free, there is no longer male and female; for all of you are one in Christ Jesus." Fifth, debate over the interpretation of specific words, for example, 'headship,' may refer to the 'source' of one's life rather than 'authority' over one's life (Eph. 5:23; 1 Cor. 11:3); cf. mutual submission found in Eph. 5:21. Finally, if the subordination of women is thought to be due to the fall of humanity into sin, then that curse should be overturned, just as Christians have sought to overturn other curses, for example, making it easier to grow crops, or to ease the pain of childbirth (see Genesis 3:8-21).

Final Comments

What makes people unique? That is a tough question, which scientists as well as Christians have had difficulty answering. No doubt we will continue to learn more about what it means to be human as scientists and behavioral scientists do more research, and as Christians consider those findings in relationship to their beliefs, values, and practices.

Human beings are, of course, different from each other. We identify with different genders, races, cultural groups, nationalities, religions, and more. It is important to remember that just because we are different does not mean that our differences are always a basis for hierarchical assessment. Human beings are complementary to each other—our differences make us better together than we are apart. But just because we are complementary doesn't mean that one kind of person deserves more power than another. We can be complementarian, for example, without being patriarchal.

In the meantime, Christians maintain that people are more than their physical and biological makeup. If people are to be understood, respected, and treated justly, then we must also consider their spiritual state, which reflects God's image in which they were created. Thus, all people should be viewed and treated as inherently valuable, worthy of love.

The Problem of Evil

There is a famous conversation between two brothers in Fyodor Dostoevsky's novel *The Brothers Karamazov*, which epitomizes what has become known as the problem of evil. The conversation occurs between Alyosha, who believed in God and trained for the priesthood, and his brother Ivan, who deeply struggled with belief in God due to the extent of evil, pain, and suffering in the world. In particular, Ivan lamented the torture of innocent children in Russia, some of whom had been brutalized to death, or thrown alive to be devoured by dogs. Ivan acknowledged that many adults understandably suffer for their transgressions, but that the same was not true for the youngest of children. From his perspective, the suffering of even one innocent child called into question the legitimacy of belief in an all-powerful and loving God.

Most people in life have experienced enough suffering in their own lives, or they are sufficiently aware of it in the lives of others, to empathize with the frustration and questions that arise from the belief in God in a world in which evil, sin, pain, and suffering exist. Christians as well as non-Christians have admitted that the problem of evil represents probably the greatest hurdle for them, intellectually and existentially, in how they understand God or relate to God.

Of course, one could argue that the problem of evil only exists for those who believe in God. If God does not exist, then what is the problem? If there is no God, then are not pain and suffering merely a matter of bad luck? After all, is not the concept of evil a religious term, which has no place in a scientific or evolutionary worldview? In my opinion, however, everyone is instinctively aware of, and as a matter of conscience is sensitive to, widespread pain and suffering. It is incumbent upon Christians to attempt answers to heartfelt questions that arise, if they expect to have integrity in sharing about their understanding of God.

Formulating the Issues

The logical problem of evil goes back, at least, to the time of the Greek philosopher Epicurus. With regard to belief in God, he posited the problem of evil by stating three unresolvable propositions:

God is all-powerful.
God is all-loving.
Evil exists.

Either God is powerful, but not sufficiently loving to overcome evil, or God is loving, but not sufficiently powerful to overcome evil. One could deny that evil exists, but that prospect would deny all the pain and suffering people experience.

From a logical perspective, Christians have argued that their belief in God is not unreasonable. Instead, it is argued that the logic of the problem has been stated unfairly. An alternative understanding of the problem may be viewed as follows:

God is all-powerful and all-loving.
Evil exists.
There is a morally sufficient reason for why evil exists.

The question remains: What is the morally sufficient reason for why evil exists?

In church history, several explanations for why evil exists have arisen, but there is no consensus among Christians. These explanations have been described as examples of theodicy (Gk., *theos*, 'God' + *dike*, 'justice, right') — arguments for the righteousness and goodness of an almighty God in a world in which evil exists.

Some Christians have helpfully made distinctions between what a theodicy accomplishes. Is it a rational (and empirical) proof, or is it a reasonable defense? Similar to arguments for God's existence, I do not expect that arguments for the righteousness and goodness of an almighty God in a world in which evil exists will convince many people, at least, not based only upon rational and empirical argumentation. Because Christianity is based on faith, and not on clear-sightedness — rationally and empirically — Christians only need to show the reasonableness of their faith, rather than provide propositional argumentation, which probably will die the death of a thousand qualifications. Although faith consists of rational and empirical components, it has as much or more to do with relational, moral, or trust issues that people have with God. So,

78

let us look at some traditional theodicies that have arisen in church history in order to understand better their understanding of the reasonableness of their Christian belief in God, in a world in which evil exists.

Theodicies

Several theodicies have been presented as attempts to provide morally sufficient reasons for why an all-powerful and all-loving God would create a world in which evil, sin, pain, and suffering occur. The most prominent theodicy is the free will defense, most often associated with Augustine. Augustine did not believe that God created evil. Instead, evil represents a privation or corruption of God's good creation, especially by people. After people acted sinfully, God justly punished them. Thereafter, people inherit from one another an in-built propensity to sin, since the origination of sin, which leaves people morally corrupt and totally in need of God's gracious aid in order to save them from damnation.

Although people are blamed for sin, it is not clear how an all-powerful and all-loving God would not have foreseen the evil and sin of people, and thus bear implicit responsibility for them. Blaming Satan does not resolve the problem of evil, since Satan is thought to have been a creation of God, just like people. So, you can push the free will theodicy to a time before the creation of people, but it does not resolve the question of why God allows evil to occur in the world.

An alternative soul-making theodicy is associated with the second century bishop Irenaeus. Soul-making theodicy acknowledges that God knew that people would succumb to evil and sin, through the abuse of their free will. But people can only exercise truly the image of God, in which they were created, if they live in a world in which good does not always win, and in which evil sometimes does. People can only learn to develop faith, hope, and love (as well as wisdom, moderation, justice, courage, and other virtues) where they have to struggle and persevere, intellectually as well as in other ways.

It makes sense that the quality of a soul requires a context in which people are challenged physical, morally, and spiritually. However, there seem to occur instances of evil and sin that do not provide any opportunity for growth, that is, that there is no discernable teleological end. Random acts of violence, for example, or pain and suffering imposed upon the youngest of children do not seem conducive to growth in character. In addition, some instances of evil and sin seem excessive, again not providing opportunities for people in extreme occurrences of pain and suffering to learn from them.

These theodicies may not satisfy all questions and concerns related to belief in an all-powerful and all-loving God in a world in which evil exists. But they are intended to give plausible explanations for the beliefs that Christians have. For most people, the problem of evil is not so much an intellectual problem as it is a problem of lived experience; it is an existential problem related to their physical, emotional, and relational well-being. Theodicies may begin to help them explain why they have faith, but the vitality of their faith involves more than rational and empirical argumentation.

O Felix Culpa

There are several commonalities that occur among Christian theodicies. Probably the most significant can be summed up by an ancient hymn, which begins with the words *O felix culpa* (Lat., 'oh fortunate crime' or 'oh happy fall'). The argument is that a greater good occurs if people are given the freedom to choose, even if some choose what is evil, than to have never been given the freedom to choose. If people had been created without freedom to choose, then their lives would have been robotically programmed. Likewise, if people had been created without freedom to choose, then how could they experience love—the highest Christian virtue? A measure of mutuality is required for love to occur between two people.

Even if there are basic differences between people, for example, between a parent and a child, or between God and people, then there needs to be ongoing freedom that genuinely allows people to choose. Although God risks, so to speak, that not all people might choose to believe in, relate with, or love God, a greater good occurs when people have freedom, despite the occurrence— sometimes without an apparent purpose, and sometimes excessively—of evil, sin, pain, and suffering.

Friedrich Leibnitz proposed a theodicy, claiming that we live in 'the best of all possible worlds.' To his critics, Leibnitz's theodicy seemed laughable, if not horrifying. It does not take much imagination, critics argued, to imagine a better world than the one in which we live: less pain? more pleasure? But Leibnitz argued that, given all the possible worlds that God could have created — with greater and lesser degrees of human freedom allowable — we live in the best proportioned context for God's goodness and love as well as power to be manifest for the sake of people. Although one may imagine better circumstances in any given situation, Leibnitz argued that creation as a whole — for all people, for all times and places — is the best of all possible worlds.

Cruciality of Jesus

No theodicy, no defense of the goodness and love of God, would be complete without looking at the person, life, death, and resurrection of Jesus. It may seem obvious that this would be the case, and yet in times of pain and suffering, people do not always look often enough at Jesus. As Scripture says, God empathized with and cared so much about the problems of evil, sin, pain, and suffering that God came to earth. God came to earth in the person of Jesus in order to identify and suffer with people, and to provide an ultimate way of escape from the finitude of human life as well as from the effects of sin, death, and condemnation.

The promise of eternal life may not seem sufficient for all the evil, sin, pain, and suffering that occurs, and I am not saying that it is. There is really no way to dismiss, in my opinion, the injustices, violence, catastrophe, weeping, and sorrow people experience. But what I can affirm is that God did not leave us to experience pain and suffering alone. God was with us in the past, though the life, death, and resurrection of Jesus, and God continues to be with us in the present, though the person and work of the Holy Spirit. We are not alone, and we do not suffer alone. We may feel alone, abandoned, and destitute, but we are never truly alone. God is with us — comforting, encouraging, guiding, and empowering us to persevere.

Christian churches are more involved with ministry to those who hurt, than they are involved with apologetics. God does not call upon Christians so much to answer the problem of evil, as it is called upon to minister to those who suffer injustices, violence, catastrophe, weeping, and sorrow. The problem of evil will no doubt, in this world, continue to perplex people intellectually and existentially. In the meantime, Christians and churches will continue to proclaim the whole gospel of Jesus, which ministers to more than people's eternal well-being but also to their immediate this-worldly needs — as Jesus ministered to people.

Final Comments

In this life, we may not find answers to every question and concern that we have. With regard to the problem of evil, there remain tough issues that pertain to the sometimes pointless and excessive suffering that people experience. We may not, in this life, be able to answer all the questions and concerns about God that Ivan had in *The Brothers Karamazov*, especially concerning the suffering of innocent children. And yet, if there is no God, then do answers become easier with which to cope?

Christians consider faith in God as all-powerful and all-loving, despite the presence of evil and its effects, to be a reasonable faith. But it is still a matter of faith. We must entrust our lives to God, believing that in life hereafter — if not also increasingly in this life — the benefits of salvation and of becoming reconciled with God outweigh the alternatives, even as we fight to alleviate the evil, sin, pain, and suffering they cause.

Sin, Ignorance, Misery, and Bondage

Imagine a pastor being asked to respond to a married couple, who admitted that they were experiencing marital problems. Would you imagine that the pastor would ask: What sin is causing these problems? No, of course not. Most pastors would instead ask: How are your communication skills? How might your different upbringings affect how you relate to one another in marriage? The topic of sin might come up eventually, but in practice, most pastors realize that challenges that people experience in life may have multiple causes, and not just sin per se. Similar things could be said about problems that people experience with their parenting, finances, work, or other areas of life.

One of the crucial contributions that Christianity offers in understanding the breadth and depth of human problems has to do with sin, which has caused them to be estranged from God, and which has impaired other aspects of their lives. Without remedying this spiritual dimension of people's lives, they will never experience wholeness, joy, peace, and other benefits, at least, that Scripture describes as being God's will for them.

Tom Oden talks about different views of Jesus' atonement that have distinctive perspectives about the nature of the human predicament. They include sin, ignorance, misery, and bondage. I think that these terms help us to begin to understand the breadth and depth of human problems. Although sin may represent the biblical term that most crucially needs to be dealt with in becoming reconciled with God for their salvation, other factors need to be considered with regard to what challenges people's day to day lives. A theology that only deals with the problem of sin may fail to treat the full context of problems that people experience. This is why Jesus' ministry involved more than proclaiming the gospel; it also involved discipling his followers, healing the sick, caring for the poor, and casting out demons.

What Is Sin?

Sin has variously been described as the breaking of God's laws, idolatrous disregard for God, prideful self-centeredness, personal rebellion against God, disbelief in God, or passive indifference to God. It may involve acts of commission (things we do), or omission (things we don't do), for the sake of what is right, just, and good. People sin individually and collectively, and in fact, Scripture makes no distinction between personal and social sin, since what one person does is inextricably bound up with others. In Scripture, God punished many for the sins of one person; there is no such thing as a private sin. In the Old Testament, Israel suffered due to the sinfulness of Achan (Joshua 6:15-7:15), and it suffered numerous times due to the sinfulness of Israelite kings.

Historically, Christians have talked about an original or first sin, dating back to Adam and Eve. Although not all Christians consider Adam and Eve to be historical people, who lived six thousand years ago, Christians still talk about an original or first sin happening at some time, when people reached an awareness of accountability in relationship with God. Because of that original sin, humanity has suffered since that time, both because of the natural consequences of their individual and collective sins, and because of punishments God placed upon them, again, both individually and collectively. As such, Scripture describes all people as being tainted, at least, if not totally depraved. Christians tend to agree regarding the extent of sin, believing that it impacts every aspect of their lives, but disagree regarding its depth, that is, how thoroughly sinful people are. While it is easy to describe mass murderers and torturers as totally depraved, it is not as easy to describe newborn babies or heroically virtuous people in the same way.

Even if people are born with a sin nature or predilection to sin, to what extent are they guilty of sin? Do they inherit the guilt of their ancestors' sin? Some Christians argue that babies are born just as guilty of sin as the worst people imaginable, arguing further that their eternal destiny is predetermined before they are born. However, most Christians tend to argue that babies, children, and also adults first need to reach an age of accountability (or an age of reason) before God holds them accountable for the guilt of their spiritual, relational, and moral decision-making. This accountability is due to the measure of freedom God gives people by grace to

84

choose – to accept of things related to God, or to reject them. God indeed holds them accountable for their sins, and they are born with numerous challenges to righteous, just, and good decision-making. The sinfulness of people individually is inextricably thought to be bound up with the sinfulness of people collectively, even though Scripture does not clearly explain the interconnectedness. Even so, Scripture describes all people as sinful, one way or another, and in need of forgiveness, which only God can provide for their salvation from the effects of sin, in this life and life beyond death.

Like the problem of evil previously discussed, many do not like to talk about sin. It seems unfair, they might say, or it seems psychologically archaic. Yet, in trying to understand people in-depth, Christians believe that Scripture's talk about sin provides an inescapable insight into who people are. They are people created by God, and yet they are lamentably out of relationship with God – a relationship that needs to be restored, if they want to experience fully who they are, why they exist, and how they may best live.

Ignorance, Misery, and Bondage

Jesus ministered to more than people's sin. Jesus also walked with people and lead them, making his disciples. This "discipling" shows us how God cares holistically about the quality of our lives. Jesus also ministered to the poor, the sick, those held captive, those treated unjustly, and others who suffered pain, marginalization, and oppression, of various sorts. In addition, Jesus set free those who were subject to demonic bondage or bondage to other powers, for example, those who defiled temple worship through their business dealings or maintenance of the religious status quo.

While being crucified, Jesus strikingly said, "Father, forgive them; for they do not know what they are doing" (Luke 23:24). It is usually thought that sin also had an impact on first century leaders' decisions to crucify Jesus, but in a moment of magnanimity, Jesus acknowledged that people are affected by ignorance as well as sin. As Jesus discipled his followers, he made sure to teach them, and exhorted his followers to teach others, if they want to embody the fullness of Jesus' example to them. How might church ministries differ today if Christians sought to overcome people's ignorance as much as their sin?

Teach
Model
Empower

So much of Jesus' ministry was directed toward the alleviation of people's physical pain, and of their various impoverishments. Yes, people suffered spiritually; they also suffered from disease, injury, neglect, marginalization, oppression, and violence. Throughout church history, Christians have been inconsistent in their emulation of Jesus' holistic ministry to people. Recently, social gospel and liberation theologies have reminded Christians that Jesus came to minister to people physically as well as spiritually, and collectively as well as individually. Jesus came to liberate people from sin, but also from the corporeal misery they experience, along with their ignorance and various forms of bondage.

Christians sometimes seem ambivalent about Jesus' deliverance of people from demons, or from Satan. Either they minimize that ministry for today, or ignore it altogether, perhaps demythologizing it. Yet, Jesus regularly delivered people from what is called possession or, at least, demonic oppression. Such ministries are still needed today, though admittedly, great discernment and caution need to be used in going about deliverance ministries. Equally important are deliverance ministries from other things that bind people. Bondage may be to addictions—biological, psychological, or cultural—that people have to alcohol, drugs, eating, sex, and love. It may also be to addictions that people have collectively, for example, racial discrimination, sex or gender prejudice, and bigotry of various sorts directed against those who are different—who are 'other'—due to class, sexual orientation, language, nationality, or religion.

No Sin but Social Sin

Social gospel and liberation theologies have done a great service to Christianity, reminding us of the holistic ministries that Jesus embodied and proclaimed in his gospel. Liberation theologies from developing and impoverished countries have been especially poignant in pointing out collective or societal injustices perpetrated, not only against people within one's community, but also around the world. Nations have done immense injustice against other countries through their military conquests, colonial or territorial oppression, and ongoing economic imperialism that hamstrings third world countries in a variety of ways. Collective injustices are

86

no less culpable, nor excusable, when perpetuated by Christians or by purportedly Christian-oriented countries, if indeed any country as a whole can claim to be Christian.

In the gospel of Matthew, Jesus ends his last public sermon with a parable about the judgment of the nations (Matthew 25:31-46). Of course, reference to the 'nations' does not mean that he excluded the judgment of individuals. At the very end of his ministry, when Jesus sent forth his disciples in preparation for his own leaving from this earth, Jesus said:

> Go therefore and make disciples of all nations," and he included the going of Christians to people individually as well as nations collectively – of peoples, of groups other than one's own – in this commissioning (Matthew 28:19).

In Matthew 25, Jesus says that those who neglect the "hungry...thirsty...stranger...naked...and [those] in prison" will be "accursed" (vv. 41-46). On the other hand, Jesus says that when people minister to the needs of impoverished people, it is as if they were ministering to Jesus, and will be "blessed" and "inherit the kingdom" prepared for them by God (vv. 31-40). Although there is never complete agreement with regard to how parables are to be interpreted, most Christians take seriously Jesus' message to care for people's physical and social needs, and not just for their spiritual and individual needs.

Sin Obsessions?

Sometimes Christians seem to become obsessed with specific sins. They usually seem to be individual transgressions, perhaps even sexual sins. Possibly this is a western phenomenon, influenced by individualistic emphases and preoccupations with sexuality. Certainly, Scripture talks about individuals and about sexuality, but Christians may become obsessed with certain behaviors, especially those that are not as prominent – or, at least, are not thought to be – within their particular family, tribe, or nation. For example, the sexual sin du jour that many Christians fret over is homosexuality. Although Scripture talks a little bit about homosexuality, it talks a lot more about divorce, remarriage, and adultery. When Christians focus so much upon denouncing homosexual behavior and not about what Scripture says about divorce, remarriage, and adultery, they do not realize how hypocritical they look in discriminating against just one perceived sin, and not against others. They might say that they consider divorce, remarriage, and adultery—at least, in some circumstances—to be sinful. However, they are permissive of such culturally acceptable sins, but not those that are culturally unacceptable, perhaps due more to their phobias or partisan politics than to Scripture.

When Christians obsess over certain sins, and not others, there is no way that the world can think of them as being anything other than hypocrites. It does not help that their obsessions may be more influenced by their phobias or partisan politics, or by their privileged status in society (due to their wealth, race, or ethnicity). It is no wonder that criticisms of Christians' hypocrisy and discrimination seem to be on the rise, both in terms of how churches victimize minority groups and in terms of how they are involved in narrow-minded political affairs. Christians constantly need to stop and assess the degree to which they remain faithful to Scripture, or whether they have succumbed to cultural pressures that emphasize money, power, and prestige more than gospel values.

Final Comments

In counseling people who suffer, sin ought not to be neglected in how we diagnose and provide healing for what ails them. Certainly, sin has crippled people in many ways. My daughter Liesl, who has experience in counseling, reminds me of the need for holistic healing: body and spirit, mind and emotions, individual and collective. Fortunately, God has provided a way for people to be restored, which involves holistic healing both now and for eternity.

So, we ought not to forget that Jesus' words, life, and ministry provide for people's suffering here and now. Whether people suffer from sin, ignorance, misery, or bondage—of various sorts—they need to be loved and cared for in all ways that they suffer. Jesus did no less, and those who claim to follow him should give comparable attention in ministering to all the pain and suffering that people experience.

Part Four

"That He Gave His Only Son"

God with Us

When I was young, I felt pressure when I attended church to give the appearance of being happy all the time, to be outgoing, and over-all to look good, or at least, good enough to attend church. But I was not always happy or unoccupied. Even when I was happy, I did not always look happy. I am not an extrovert; nor am I an emotionally expressive person. So, for me, just being normal seemed to make me suspect among some of the churchgoers I met. They would ask: What's wrong? Are you all right? May I pray for you? Going to church could stress me out because I did not always know — or could pull off — an outward veneer that satisfied people I met at church.

Moreover, I can remember how off-putting it was for me to hear people quote the verses: "Rejoice always, pray without ceasing, give thanks in all circumstances" (1 Thessalonians 5:16-18). Was I really supposed to rejoice and be happy all the time? What does it mean to pray without ceasing? And realistically, how could I give thanks in all circumstances? It seemed impossible to fulfill these expectations privately, much less publicly. Seeming insurmount-able, why try at all to be Christian?

When I looked at Jesus in Scripture, however, I felt encouraged. Regardless of how you view him, Jesus repeatedly exhibited pain, suffering, and tearfulness in his life. He wept over the death of his friend Lazarus. Jesus spent long nights praying alone, and in the Garden of Gethsemane, before his arrest and crucifixion, the gospel of Matthew 26 describes Jesus as being "grieved and agitated" (v. 37), "deeply grieved, even to death" (v. 38), and throwing himself on the ground, prayed, "let this cup pass from me" (v. 39). If that is what is meant by rejoicing all the time, then I could do that! If Jesus modeled giving thanks in all circumstances, then I could handle that as well, since he showed me a more realistic example of godly living, since he did not seem always to be smiling and cheery either. My problem in church was that, too often, verses would be selected from Scripture and be applied (or implied) through preaching and teaching in ways that discouraged people, more than encouraged them, for living as Christians.

While Jesus lived on earth, he lived as we live—relying upon the Holy Spirit for help—in being and doing all that God wanted of him. Paradoxically, Christians believe that Jesus was divine, but that he did not live by relying upon his innate divinity. Jesus lived in a finite world, tainted by sin, as we live. So, he provides for us, among other things, a convincing picture of how we are to live, without the admixture of unrealistic expectations that Christians and churches sometimes project upon people.

Why Did God Become Human?

Most Christians in church history believe that Jesus became human, that is, incarnate (from the Latin *incarno*, 'to make into flesh' or, 'to be made flesh'), in order to save people from sin and death, and to provide for their reconciliation with God and eternal life in heaven. John 3:16 certainly suggests this key component of the gospel. Jesus satisfied all that was required for people to live eternally. But Jesus provided much more!

In the Middle Ages, a Benedictine monk named Anselm wrote *Cur Deus Homo* (Lat., *Why God Became a Man*). In addition to talking about how Jesus satisfied all divine requirements for people's salvation, Anselm talked about Jesus' relevance for us here and now. Perhaps the most important reason for why God became human in the person of Jesus was to provide people with a role model for how they ought to live. Jesus did not blithely live life without problems: hunger and other basic human needs, responsibilities to family and ministry, taxes to a colonizing empire, and other trials—personal and social—that we also face. Jesus was tempted to sin, criticized by religious and political leaders, betrayed by friends, and tortured mercilessly. He also died, thus experiencing to the fullest the challenges that plague people every day.

Being a follower of Jesus is not always easy. Even Jesus warned his followers of this reality. Yet Jesus gives us a realistic role model for how we ought to live. He not only provides a role model for us as individuals, but also how we ought to live collectively in society as well as in churches. As individuals, we should be encouraged for a more realistic picture of what the Christian life is like—with its benefits as well as challenges—than what is sometimes skewed by Christians and churches.

Not Accepting the Status Quo

Jesus was not content to accept the status quo of social problems. He aided the poor—those impoverished in many ways. Jesus both showed compassion for the needs people experienced, and he advocated for changing the causes of their impoverishment. Jesus repeatedly critiqued leaders in ancient Israel who contributed to the impoverishment of others, whether it be through unjust temple practices, hypocritical neglect of the poor, misuse of Scripture for hiding their self-indulgence, or unfair tax collection. He was regularly challenged and maligned by religious leaders, since Jesus did not perpetuate the status quo. Instead Jesus wanted to progress beyond the existing state of affairs, implementing social as well as religious changes that benefited people holistically, and not just spiritually.

For example, Jesus challenged the status quo of many of the social, political, and economic practices of his day. Like Amos in the Old Testament, Jesus challenged unjust practices of leaders, who neglected and oppressed the people they ruled. In relationship to an evildoer, Jesus advocated neither 'fight' nor 'flight,' but a third way of challenging the injustices of violent oppression. In his Sermon on the Mount, Jesus disregarded the old wisdom of demanding an "eye for an eye, and a tooth for a tooth"—the old *lex talonis*, Lat., 'law of retaliation' (Matthew 5:38). Instead, he advocated another way of non-violent resistance, which neither succumbed to violence-for-violence nor succumbed to letting injustice go unopposed. Jesus said: "But I say to you, Do not resist an evildoer. But if anyone strikes you on the right cheek, turn the other also" (Matthew 5:39). In other words, actively oppose injustice so that people may be liberated from those who oppress them, even though advocacy against injustice occurs in non-violent ways.

In relationship to the Roman colonialists, who would oppress common Israelites by demanding that they carry soldiers' cloaks for a mile, Jesus challenged such injustices. Again, he challenged them not through fight or flight, but by going the extra-mile—so to speak—in publicly challenging the harassment of soldiers' demands. For example, when imposing upon commoners to carry a garment for a mile, Jesus exhorted his followers to "go also the second mile" (Matthew 5:41). The extra mile was more a protest against the unjust demand than it was evidence of docile acquiescence. Carrying a cloak one mile satisfied imperial subjugation, but carrying it a second mile represented non-violent act of civil disobedience by actively resisting against the oppressive practices of both individual soldiers and governments.

Jesus was a role model for non-violent civil disobedience. But his political activism is overlooked by many Christians and churches, who are sometimes more heavily invested in maintaining the status quo of society, and in preserving their privileged status within it, rather than in righting social injustices.

Meaning of *Kenosis*

What does it mean for Jesus to serve as our role model? Was he not God? How can we follow Jesus, if he was in any way divine, and we are not? Is that not an impossible standard? Why even try to follow Jesus' example?

In Philippians 2:7, the apostle Paul talks about Jesus as having "emptied himself" (Gk., *kenosis*) of divinity in order to become human. Christians have queried over this passage for centuries. For the most part, Christians have tended to believe that Jesus' divine-human nature ultimately transcends human understanding, and so a degree of mystery in describing God is inevitable.

The question remains: To what degree did Jesus genuinely live and make decisions as we must do so today? Some Christians have thought that Jesus lived more by divine attributes than by human attributes, and thus his role model serves more as a goal to be pursued than achieved. In practice, however, most have viewed Jesus as a realistic role model to follow. He really did live as we must live, relying upon the person and work of the Holy Spirit, rather than upon intrinsic power to do so, whether it be divine or human. When Jesus prayed, he did so, not just to serve as a role model, but because he—through the Holy Spirit—needed comfort, encouragement, guidance, and empowerment. People today need the same help from the Holy Spirit.

Jesus also gives Christians and churches a corrective for how they should live counter culturally in the world. He did not come to maintain the status quo, but to change it by challenging the beliefs, values, and practices of Judaism, even if it meant challenging the authority of its leaders and historic traditions. Did Jesus usher in a new status quo? No, because the church was a living reality made up of Christians, who needed to develop, maintain, and reform — when needed — the life and ministries of churches, which were to model themselves after the holistic life and ministries of Jesus. He did not come to earth to restrict and exclude people from the gospel. Instead Jesus came to welcome and include people, as well as to heal them from all that causes pain and suffering. As such, following Jesus' example as a role model for us today is the worst-best experience you will ever have. Following Jesus' example means emptying ourselves of the things that get in the way of our loving and serving others, just as Jesus did.

Fullness of Why God Became Human

Jesus came to save people from sin and death, and he came to provide a role model for how we should live. Jesus also did more! In this life, he revealed more to us about God than had previously been known. Jesus revealed God as a loving father, as a loving parent, given the best of what we know about parenting. He emphasized the love of God for people, and how love ought to be the foremost virtue of God's followers.

Jesus also revealed that he will serve as people's ultimate judge. But he will be a just judge, and an empathetic judge, since Jesus lived as we live. Hebrews 4:15 says:

> For we do not have a high priest who is unable to empathize with our weaknesses." As such, we may "approach God's throne of grace with confidence" (Hebrews 4:16).

Jesus as high priest continues to work in our lives through the Holy Spirit. We are not alone; we are never alone. In one way or another, God is always present — through Jesus establishing our salvation, and through the Holy Spirit completing our salvation. We do not need to fear the future, nor our present life and its inevitable challenges. Again, we are not alone!

Scripture also tells us that, by becoming human in Jesus, God provided the means by which to overcome demonic bondage. In his life, Jesus actively cast out sins. After his death, resurrection, and ascension, Jesus made it possible through the Holy Spirit that his followers no longer need fear spiritual bondage to demons or to Satan. First John 3:8 suggests that it was Jesus' purpose "to destroy the works of the devil." This does not mean, however, that Christians are no longer susceptible to demonic and Satanic temptation, or of spiritual oppression.

Christians have different opinions regarding the degree to which they ought to be involved with spiritual warfare: Some believe that they actively need to pray for angels in celestial battle against demons and Satan; others believe that demons have more persuasive power over them, rather than coercive power. When it comes to discerning Christians' view of spiritual warfare, however, how they live in practice often reveals more about what they truly believe, than by what they say.

In sum, the presence of demons and Satan certainly complicate our lives, individually and collectively. However, we probably have more to fear from our own decision-making and from the influence of others, rather than from that of demons and Satan.

Final Comments

Can we be like Jesus, which reflects the original meaning of the word Christian — being a Christ-follower? If I am to be like Jesus in the Garden of Gethsemane, then yes, I (and you) can be like Jesus. Contrary to verses that suggest that I need to be perfect — always rejoicing and always giving thanks — to be a Christian, God accepts me as I am. Since all are saved by grace through faith, we may have confidence in coming to God, both now and in eternity.

In the meantime, we should model our lives after Jesus. But this may seem like an impossible challenge, since he so often is depicted by Christians and churches in half-finished ways: Spiritual only? Meek only? Blasé only? On the contrary, the role model Jesus left us was advocative both for our spiritual well-being and for our physical well-being. He was spiritually counter cultural and also physically, socially, politically, and economically counter-cultural. Christ-followers would do well to consider, embody, and advocate on behalf of others for every way in which they are impoverished.

At-One-Ment with God

When my daughters were young, there were house rules. As a parent, I needed to set boundaries for home life. For example, my daughters did not have the freedom to take cookies out of the cookie jar without permission. If they took a cookie without permission, then stealing occurred. If a daughter was caught stealing, then there would be consequences. This is not because I wanted to discipline my daughters, but because I wanted to instill in them a sense of responsibility, of justice, and of character development with regard to family relations and home boundaries.

If a daughter was caught stealing, then it was not enough for me—as her father—to hear a confession. A confession may not reflect a contrite heart and accountability to one another; instead, a confession may only reflect the fact that she was caught. What I wanted to hear from a daughter was sorrow for having transgressed a rule, resolve not to steal again, and realization that a personal betrayal had damaged her relationship with me and with the rest of the family. If healing and restoration was to occur in our relationship, then growth needed to occur in her self-awareness about justice and injustice, a desire to become reconciled with those who had been wronged, and a commitment not to steal again.

This story of cookie transgression and restoration may seem simple, and perhaps a bit humorous. But it is intended as an analogy for how God wants to become reconciled with people, who have sinned, and not just to forgive their sins. When God created the world, God set boundaries, so to speak. Within the world, God wanted people to grow through the experiences of responsibility and accountability in order to provide a context in which a quality relationship with God might develop, along with quality relationships with others.

In response to the sin and broken relationship, which aliened God from people, many stories, images, and analogies are found in Scripture to describe how God provided humanity with the opportunity for salvation—for forgiveness, healing, reconciliation, and growth, as well as for their eternal life. They represent pictures of how people may humanly understand all of what God has done to restore their relationships with one another. No single picture (story, image, or analogy) may be sufficient to describe the fullness of what Jesus sacrificed on behalf of people in order to accomplish this restoration, but together they help to communicate the full gospel to which God wants people to respond. One of the most common words used to describe God's provision for people's restoration is *atonement*.

What Is Atonement?

The early English language meaning of the word atonement implied 'at-one-ment,' that is, reconciliation between people, or between people and God. In the Old Testament, atonement had to do with people making sacrificial offerings of animals, grain, or other gifts in order to atone for their sins, that is, to make amends or reparation. This was part of the old covenant that God established with the Israelite people. In the New Testament, Jesus' sacrifice is described as the decisive atonement for people's sins (Romans 3:25; Hebrews 2:17). This was part of the new covenant God established with all people. As such, Jesus' sacrifice was considered sufficient for all time. The sacrificial system of the Old Testament was no longer necessary, because a new covenant of grace and faith was inaugurated.

Sometimes Christians describe the doctrine of atonement as the *objective* dimension of salvation, having to do with what God accomplished in the past for people's salvation now. Since people cannot earn or merit salvation, God needed to provide that which was objectively needed through the life, death, and resurrection of Jesus. In addition to the objective provision for salvation by God, it remains for the subjects (that is, people) to receive or accept God's provision. This *subjective* dimension of salvation has to do with how individual people respond to or believe in God's provision here and now for their salvation — for their at-one-ment with God.

Scripture uses several words, images, and analogies for describing what God has done for people's salvation. For example, words used include salvation, sacrifice, forgiveness, reconciliation, expiation (removing that which separates people from God), and propitiation (providing that which reconciles people with God). Throughout church history, other words have been used, such as satisfaction, substitution, liberation, and others. Problems have arisen when Christians and churches insist on one particular word, image, or analogy to describe God's atonement for people, to the exclusion of others. This reductionist approach extinguishes the holistic nature of the atonement described in Scripture. Looking at the variety of biblical (and extra-biblical) words helps to capture a broader understanding of God's workings in people's lives, both in the past for atonement and for people's present salvation.

Views of the Atonement

The way that Christians in the early church talked about the atonement was the ransom view. Jesus was described as being a ransom by which people would be saved (e.g., 1 Timothy 2:6). It was not entirely clear, however, how this biblical language was to be understood. Was the ransom paid to God? to Satan? In later times, this view of the atonement became known as *Christus Victor* (Lat., 'Christ the victor') because Jesus was thought to have overpowered all that bind people—spiritually, demonically, and in all ways. Jesus victoriously overpowered all that holds people in bondage.

During the Middle Ages, Anselm talked about atonement as satisfaction, since Jesus satisfied all of God's requirements for salvation, regardless of how one understood satisfaction. Satisfaction could refer to a sacrificial requirement by God, legal requirement that needs rectification, or requirement of a courtly honor due to God (working within metaphors that would have made sense to a medieval monk!). During the Reformation, Protestants such as Calvin advocated that satisfaction be understood as Jesus' substitution (or penal substitution) for humanity. In this regard, Jesus is thought to have paid the legal price for sin (Galatians 3:13-15). This analogy became very popular, but it does not represent all of the biblical imagery for atonement.

Abelard, also during the Middle Ages, emphasized the moral influence of Jesus' atoning role. Rather than focusing on the objective basis for salvation, Abelard thought that Jesus provided a role model for how people ought to live morally and spiritually, indicative of a Christ-like life. From this perspective, Jesus' atonement puts more emphasis on how we ought to live here and now (the subjective dimension of atonement), rather than upon what Jesus did in the past (the objective dimension of the atonement). Thus, Abelard placed emphasis upon people's subjective experience (or reception, acceptance) of the gospel today, rather than focusing on what God accomplished in the past for salvation.

After the Reformation, Hugo Grotius advocated a governmental view of the atonement, agreeing that Jesus served as a substitute on behalf of people, but that it was more than a simple act of substitution. Technically, God did not need a substitution; God did not require a blood sacrifice in order to forgive humanity. God could have commuted the sins of humanity, without the need for violent crucifixion in order to satisfy God's justice. Like a loving parent, God does not require corporeal punishment in order for children to become reconciled with God. Rather, Jesus sacrificed his life on behalf of people in order to show that God's moral government (or standards) remained intact. Even though God's salvation is a gift, God still wants believers to act morally; they should not think that God's gift gives them license to act any way they want. Through Jesus' obedience on the cross, God reaffirmed the goodness of biblical commands and principles, and for how believers ought to live holy, loving, and just lives.

Contemporary Views

Contemporary words, images, and analogies for the atonement are sometimes advocated by Christians. These are attempts either to distill biblical truths sometimes overlooked, or to provide insightful means by which to communicate God's gift of salvation today. For example, some Christians appeal to the notion of liberation, saying that God liberated people from sin and death, just as God wants to liberate them from sickness, poverty, and injustice. Liberation theology, for example, draws an analogy between the Old Testament (and old covenant) and the New Testament (and new covenant): God first liberated the Israelites from slavery by means of the Exodus, and then God liberated Israelites — indeed, all people — through Jesus' atonement. As such, Christians should seek to liberate all, proclaiming the gospel in word and deed, freeing people from all that enslaves them, physically as well as spiritually. This kind of atonement theology puts a great emphasis on the holistic nature of Jesus' salvation.

Some Christians talk about salvation in terms of therapeutic healing. Just as people fell into sin, incurably tainting the image of God in which they were created, God sent Jesus in order to heal them spiritually and also physically, individually and also collectively. In biblical times, the word *therapeia* (Gk., 'cure, therapy, remedy') was thought of in terms of holistic healing, and not just psychological therapy or healing, as it is usually thought of today. Jesus' healing ministry included the spiritual well-being of people as well as their physical well-being.

Christians are sometimes creative, using present-day cultural stories, songs, movies, and other social media for communicating Jesus' atonement in ways that might be more understandable and compelling to people today. For example, Christians have used stories about self-sacrifice and bridges over troubled water, songs about forgiveness and lighting up another's life, and even science fiction movies have provided Christians with culturally up-to-date ways of talking about Jesus' atonement. These stories creatively help to communicate the many biblical words, images, and analogies for communicating a spiritual and eternal reality that ultimately transcends our human ability to describe fully.

It can be argued that all historic views of the atonement reflect the particular cultural context in which they became prominent. For example, the ransom view reflected an era in the ancient world that understood the common practice of kidnapping and ransoms. The satisfaction view reflected an era in the Middle Ages that understood the need for satisfying the chivalrous honor of offended nobility. The moral influence view reflected another theological perspective that desired a greater role for people in salvation, as many people experienced during the Reformation. The (penal) substitution view reflected a Protestant era in which legal affairs had become increasingly important to society. The governmental view reflected a theological perspective of the Enlightenment era that did not think God required a violent blood sacrifice in order to forgive people. Regardless of whether the aforementioned views do (or do not) reflect the particular place and time in which they became prominent, Christians need to be aware of the contextual nature of all their theological affirmations. Their contextuality does not make them relative or unreal; it merely helps us to be more aware as well as humble in what Christians claim to be true.

Global Perspectives

All around the world, Christians and churches have drawn uniquely from their respective socio-cultural contexts in order to communicate Jesus and the gospel to others. In Asia, Jesus may be viewed as a guru or avatar, and the atonement may be viewed as a peace-child exchanged between tribes in order to prevent tribal violence. In Africa, Jesus may be viewed as a medicine man, and the atonement may be viewed in the context of healing rituals.

Are these socio-cultural understandings syncretistic? Heretical? Perhaps. But not necessarily. Not all drawings from parts of the world outside of the United States and Europe effectively communicate biblical and historic Christian beliefs, values, and practices. So great care is needed in translating the gospel into other socio-cultural contexts. However, if such attempts are criticized by Christians for being contextual, and those critics do not realize or acknowledge their own socio-cultural context as well as those of past views of the atonement, then they are inconsistent, at best, and hypocritical at worst. Since theological formulations reflect the situatedness in which they arose, Christians and churches need to be open from what they may learn from the global understandings of God their own context — past and present.

Importance of Relationality

A common thread throughout all the views of atonement ultimately has to do with restoring the relationship between God and people. Salvation is personal! It is love that motivates this relationship. Of course, love begins with God. 1 John 4:19 says: "We love because he first loved us." Although there are many things that need to be attended to in restoring covenantal fellowship with God, loving God with one's whole heart, soul, mind, and strength is the *telos* — the end, the goal.

The various views of atonement talk about sacrifice, satisfaction, moral influence, substitution, governance, and more. God is thought to have provided the objective basis by which people are saved. But salvation does not deal just with the past; it also has to do with the present. In the present, people are to believe and repent; they are also expected to become personally reconciled with God, their creator, their savior, their *Abba*. We are to love God now and forever, and love requires people's choices in loving God with their whole heart, soul, mind, and strength. In addition, they are to love their neighbor — individually and collectively, locally and globally — as themselves.

Final Comments

Fortunately, the theft of cookies by my daughters was not a common problem. Like Jesus, they "increased in wisdom and in years, and in divine and human favour" (Matthew 2:52). I have good reason to feel parental pride when it comes to how I value my daughters!

One of the unique things about Christianity is that salvation comes to people, not by their own effort or merit, and not by self-enlightenment or self-actualization. Salvation is a gift, objectively provided by God through Jesus' life, death, and resurrection. Regardless of how you envision the atonement — using various words, images, and analogies — it results in reconciliation with God, with a renewed relationship that begins now and lasts forever.

God's Advocate

According to Scripture, Jesus resurrected after he was crucified. As much as the disciples rejoiced in Jesus' resurrection, its implications were difficult for them fully to grasp, both with regard to Jesus and potentially about themselves. What added to the disciples' bewilderment was Jesus' declaration that he would again leave them—that he would ascend to heaven. Why couldn't Jesus stay? Why couldn't Jesus continue to be with them to help?

Jesus had anticipated these kinds of questions, and he told his disciples in advance that it would be best if he did not always stay with them. Instead he would send an advocate (and comforter), who would be with them in spirit and power forever—the Holy Spirit. In John 16:7, Jesus says:

> I tell you the truth: it is to your advantage that I go away, for if I do not go away, the Advocate will not come to you; but if I go, I will send him to you.

In a sense, it would be as if Jesus, or at least, the spirit of Jesus, would always be with the disciples. Indeed, Jesus would always be with them through the Holy Spirit, who is the third person of the trinity. The Holy Spirit would be with the disciples more continuously and intimately than any single individual on earth could be.

It is easy to understand that Jesus' disciples would always want to have him around. But that was not possible. Nor was it helpful for the disciples (and others) in their development as people, as followers of Jesus. So, Jesus told his disciples to wait for the coming—the spiritual outpouring—of God's Holy Spirit, which happened in an event that we now call Pentecost (see Acts 2). From that time on, Jesus' followers would have the advantage of a more spiritually intimate and immediate relationship with God, who would comfort, encourage, guide, and empower people beyond anything they had previously experienced.

Of course, Jesus had experienced the Holy Spirit before, while he lived and ministered on earth. Throughout the Gospels, we read about how the Holy Spirit ministered to Jesus, guided Jesus, and empowered Jesus. He did not live on earth as God; instead, Jesus lived as a finite person, just as we live as finite people. Jesus indeed left us with a role model of the kinds of things we may accomplish in life—personally and collectively—since we live with the same Holy Spirit who empowered Jesus.

Who is this Holy Spirit? What did it mean for Jesus to call the Holy Spirit an advocate? A comforter? And more. For Christians today, talk of the Holy Spirit should be of great importance, since it is the Holy Spirit with whom they deal nowadays. Yet, historically and today, Christians have been hesitant to focus on the Holy Spirit, for a number of reasons. Perhaps it is too difficult to conceive of the Holy Spirit: Too mysterious? Too faceless? Too intangible? Let us study more about God's most intimate and personal presence with us today.

The Advocate

Jesus described the Holy Spirit as the 'advocate,' which in some translations of Scripture describes the Holy Spirit as the 'comforter.' As our advocate, the Holy Spirit works directly in and through the lives of believers, and indeed through everyone. The Holy Spirit is our constant advocate, working on behalf of people's lives—initiating, enabling, and completing divine grace within them. Scripture talks about many of the works of the Holy Spirit, and readers may be surprised at the extent that Scripture talks about them, given the relative lack of attention given to the Holy Spirit by Christians and churches.

Much of what Scripture says about the Holy Spirit has to do with the actuating of salvation in people—what Scripture sometimes refers to as the "gift of the Holy Spirit" (Acts 2:38). The Holy Spirit initiates salvation by calling people to convert, working in their lives by grace to illuminate them about matters of salvation. The Holy Spirit also enables people to believe and accept salvation, yet they must still decide for themselves. These decisions are enabled by grace, but they are not determined without people's unaffected choice for salvation. People's choice, which God has enabled, is also the reason why some may choose not to believe and not to accept salvation. Some of these salvific workings of the Holy Spirit occur dramatically in an instant; some work gradually in the context of a nurturing church. Regardless of the circumstances, at some point, people are expected to decide for themselves.

Those who are saved by grace through faith may be encouraged to know that the Holy Spirit's advocacy does not end with conversion. On the contrary, conversion is one of many stages in a more holistic understanding of salvation that continues throughout life, working to heal and restore the image of God in people. Just as God's grace through the Holy Spirit works to invite and convince people to convert to Christianity, God's grace continues to sanctify believers, which enables them to experience assurance of salvation. "Sanctification" is a theological word for all of the growth that happens in a person following the point of salvation. The Holy Spirit helps believers become more loving toward God, and more loving toward their neighbors as they love themselves. Of course, there are many moving parts in salvation, so to speak, if one is willing to see it as more than a "ticket to heaven." Salvation is about more than just being saved—salvation is about transformation. Salvation, holistically conceived, has vast implications for how God wants to transform believers into greater Christ-likeness, and how God wants to transform the world in ways that reflect all the ministries (and not just a select few) that Jesus exhorted his followers to continue on earth.

Fruit of the Spirit

Scripture talks about many ways that the Holy Spirit continues to work in and through the lives of believers. The "fruit of the Spirit" represents a way that Paul talks with regard to some of the virtues that God develops through the Holy Spirit: "love, joy, peace, patience, kindness, generosity, faithfulness, gentleness, and self-control" (Galatians 5:22-23). These virtues do not emerge miraculously, though God could do this if God chose to do so. Usually virtuous living develops as believers synergistically partner with God's Spirit in their prayer life, study of Scripture, church nurture, spiritual disciplines, and other means of grace.

Virtuous living benefits more than one's individual life. It also benefits how one relates with others in terms of showing love and compassion towards them. Virtuous living benefits how one lovingly advocates on behalf of the needs, hurts, and suffering of others. The study of virtues and vices have played a large role in the lives of Christians throughout church history, but virtues and vices have to do with more than personal peace and contentment. They have to do with implementing Jesus' teachings, commands, and principles to aid society as a whole, overcoming the injustices and impoverishments that beset people. The benefits of God's Spirit do not serve to liberate individuals only but also groups of individuals, just as Jesus reached out in ministry to groups of individuals—the poor, hungry, naked, and imprisoned.

Gifts of the Spirit

Scripture talks about gifts of the Holy Spirit, and focus upon them by Christians increased during the twentieth century, due to the rise of the Pentecostal movement. Throughout most of church history, however, Christian references to a spiritual "gift" was talked about mostly as a "charism" (*charisma*, from the Gk., *charis*, "grace"; cf. plural *charismata*, or charisms), which refers to any way that God may use Christians for the spiritual benefit of others as well as for themselves. Some Christians have the gift of a particular charism. For example, Christians may preach, teach, evangelize, administrate, give, or serve others, as God's Spirit leads and empowers them. In Scripture, there was not thought to be a definitive list of such charisms, and in fact, Christians today might find new ways of serving others that biblical authors did not imagine.

Pentecostals have a more specific understanding of spiritual gifts, believing that God uniquely gives one or more supernaturally endowed gifts to Christians, which they are to use for the sake of ministry, inside and outside churches. Some Pentecostals believe that, subsequent to conversion, Christians should seek to be baptized with (or in) the Holy Spirit, which is usually evidenced by speaking in tongues. Although not all Pentecostals require tongues speaking as demonstrable proof of Holy Spirit baptism, it is a privilege that they believe Christians may experience (and should seek) in the continuation of spiritual gifts, despite long periods in church history when the manifestation of such gifts was not widespread.

A few Christians argue that spiritual gifts, as a supernatural endowment, ceased after the first century, including many other miraculous and healing phenomena. But the majority of Christians believe that the Holy Spirit continues to work today as in biblical times, though the gifts are understood more as charisms that all Christians should manifest, as led and empowered by God's Spirit, rather than as a finite number of supernatural giftings.

Pentecostalism has done Christianity a great service in reminding Christians of the importance of focusing on the person and work of the Holy Spirit. Too often the presence and power of God in people's lives are minimized, thinking that God's present role in our lives is minor, if not altogether absent. This is a great misunderstanding of Scripture and of the Holy Spirit. Christianity should not be considered as passive place-holding, based upon an atonement achieved long ago. It is to be experienced as a dynamic, present-day relationship with God, which benefits both who we are, and how we relate with others.

Pentecost

Just how do we understand the event of Pentecost, that is, the day when the Holy Spirit became active among all people, including both Christians and non-Christians? According to Scripture, many dramatic things occurred: fire appeared on the heads of Jesus' followers, tongues speaking occurred, and more than 3,000 converted! With regard to the speaking in tongues, various interpretations among Christians have occurred. Pentecostal interpreters generally think that Jesus' followers spoke in the known languages of all the people who were present. Later tongues speaking consisted either of known languages or of angelic languages (e.g., 1 Corinthians 13:1). As such, Pentecost represented an experience to which all Christians should aspire, subsequent to conversion, known as baptism with (or in) the Holy Spirit. Thereafter, they will be endowed supernaturally with one or more spiritual gifts. Often Pentecostals talk about there being nine spiritual gifts:

> To each is given the manifestation of the Spirit for the common good. To one is given through the Spirit the utterance of wisdom, and to another the utterance of knowledge according to the same Spirit, to another faith by the same Spirit, to another gifts of healing by the one Spirit, to another the working of miracles, to another prophecy, to another the discernment of spirits, to another various kinds of tongues, to another the interpretation of tongues (1 Corinthians 12:7-11).

However, other biblical lists suggest additional spiritual gifts (see Romans 12:6-8; 1 Corinthians 12:28; Ephesians 4:11).

Non-Pentecostal interpreters think of the event of Pentecost as a unique experience, which should not necessarily be thought of as normative for everyone. A great thing happened at Pentecost in that the Holy Spirit came to earth, becoming universally and continuously present, so that God's gospel might spread more effectively as the Spirit empowered Jesus' followers. Regardless of how one interprets the events of Pentecost, they highlight how Christians nowadays minister powerfully — by the Holy Spirit — in service to God and to others.

As a final point, Pentecost represents a defining example of how the gospel was no longer thought to be for Jews alone, but for all people. This theme is repeated throughout the book of Acts, which is the story of what the first Christians did immediately following the death and resurrection of Jesus. When Jesus was about to ascend into heaven, his followers asked him eagerly about the prospect of reestablishing King David's kingdom, in the here and now. Instead, Jesus said:

> It is not for you to know the times or periods that the Father has set by his own authority. But you will receive power when the Holy Spirit has come upon you; and you will be my witnesses in Jerusalem, in all Judea and Samaria, and to the ends of the earth (Acts 1:7-8).

All the ends of the earth! The gospel was to be inclusive, not exclusive; the gospel was to be for all people, regardless of who they were. Throughout the book of Acts, story after story occurs that relates the growing pains of accepting other people — non-Jewish people, who were of other racial and ethnic backgrounds, different languages and nationalities, and so on. Of course, it can be said that Christians still struggle today with being inclusive, and yet, it is at the heart of Jesus' gospel, especially as chronicled in the book of Acts.

Final Comments

Jesus may no longer be present with us in person, and we miss him. Yet, Jesus said that we are better off with the constant presence of the Holy Spirit, rather than for him to remain physically present on earth. Why? It is because of the Holy Spirit's ongoing and immediate presence in our lives. The Holy Spirit comforts and encourages us in times of need; the Holy Spirit brings to memory Jesus and his teachings, and guides us for day to day living; and perhaps, most importantly, the Holy Spirit empowers us, giving us the grace to be, think, and act in ways that are pleasing to God and fulfilling to us.

Do you still have a difficult time visualizing the Holy Spirit? Think of Jesus, or if you prefer, the Spirit of Jesus. The Holy Spirit represents Jesus, just as much as the Holy Spirit represents God, our creator and sanctifier. So, think about Jesus' Spirit as always being with us. This same Spirit is our greatest advocate as well as comforter in life.

Scripture, Tradition, Reason, and Experience

When I began my studies in college, I took a frosh writing seminar. In it my professor would advise students individually. In one of the advisement sessions, my professor told me that I should not use so many (if any) semi-colons. He said it was bad writing style. In my defense, I said that Scripture contained semi-colons. In a matter of fact response, my professor said that he did not care if Scripture contained semi-colons; it was bad writing style. I was stunned! It was not because of my use of semi-colons, but because it was the first time in my memory that someone outside the church had so decisively (and nonchalantly) talked about Scripture being in any way 'bad.'

At the time, I used the 1611 King James Version of the Bible, which uses old-fashioned English language (for example, thee, thou). Moreover, it was not up to date with regard to modern trends in English grammar—not to mention the fact that the original languages that the Bible was written in contain no punctuation at all. Be that as it may, I had long questioned and debated with family and friends in church about Scripture's apparent inconsistencies, ranging from chronological inconsistencies in Genesis to fantastic speculations about the end times related to the book of Revelation. Scripture also did not mesh with what I was taught in school about physics, geology, biology, and the behavioral sciences. Historically, Scripture contained internal as well as external chronological discrepancies. Morally, I increasingly found ethical teachings in Scripture that were troubling: Slavery? Violence against women? War? Genocide? And these troubling teachings did not occur at the instigation of people, but of God!

Growing up, I did not attend a church that mandated a modern view of biblical perfectionism, which in its simplest manifestation claims that Scripture contains no errors, including errors about science and history. Christians who argue for the errorlessness (or inerrancy) of Scripture usually provide a long list of qualifications for what they affirm and deny about defining an error. But the presence of so many qualifications begs the question

113

further about Scripture's discrepancies. So, I studied Scripture more and more in order to decide for myself with regard to what I believe about its reliability, truthfulness, and trustworthiness. Ironically, it is not usually those who are unfamiliar with Scripture that struggle most with its truth, morality, and religious authority. Instead, it is those who study Scripture in-depth, for example, its genre, historical context, and literary context, who struggle most with its reliability. This is reminder for us to look more closely at Scripture. If we aren't troubled by the truth claims of Scripture, then we aren't reading it close enough!

Of course, Scripture did not just drop from heaven, which some Christians seem to think. Instead, it was written over hundreds of years, and it took another couple hundreds of years after Jesus lived before a canon—or standardized set of Christian Scriptures—was established. So, let us talk about some of the characteristics Christians use to describe their beliefs about Scripture.

Inspiration of Scripture

Most Christians refer to 2 Timothy 3:16 in describing Scripture as being divinely inspired:

> All Scripture is inspired by God and is useful for teaching, for reproof, for correction, and for training in righteousness, so that everyone who belongs to God may be proficient, equipped for every good work.

Some biblical translations of inspiration talk about being "God-breathed" (e.g., New International Version), which also emphasizes the divine nature of Scripture. However, subsequent descriptions of Scripture as "useful" (or "profitable," e.g., King James Version, New American Standard Version) seems underwhelming, considering lofty claims that Christians sometimes make about the perfection or errorlessness of Scripture.

Although most Christians believe in the divine inspiration of Scripture, inspiration may be understood in various ways. It may imply an absolute inspiration so that one might deduce a perfect Scripture, given the inspiration of a perfect God. However, it may also imply an inspiration of ideas, such as how a teacher inspires a student. But that does not necessarily imply a writing that is anything close to perfection. In church history, there has not been consensus about the implications of what it means for Scripture to be divinely inspired. In fact, growing historical and critical studies of Scripture point to a more modest and fallible understanding of its reliability, regardless of whether one understands Scripture primarily as a religious text, or as an equally authoritative text about science and history.

Perhaps a better word used to describe the authority of Scripture in church history is 'sufficiency,' which is a word that Christians have used in doctrinal statements to talk about the inspiration, reliability, and authority of Scripture. The word sufficiency has the advantage of being found in Scripture. For example, in talking about how his prayers for healing did not result in healing, at least, not the way he had hoped, the apostle Paul said that God instead said to him: "My grace is sufficient for you, for power is made perfect in weakness" (2 Corinthians 12:9). Although Paul was not talking about Scripture, Christians and churches have used the word sufficiency to say that we should be content with the Scripture God gave to us, and not fancy the Scripture we wish we had. After all, it would be nice to have an inerrant or infallible Scripture. But these concepts seem more like wishful thinking projected upon Scripture, which rely upon modernistic oriented arguments (e.g., inerrancy, infallibility), rather than upon familiar terms found in the biblical texts. After all, it is the Holy Spirit who moved people to speak prophetically in ways that led to the writing of Scripture (2 Peter 1:20-21). So, it is the Holy Spirit who guarantees the sufficiency of Scripture, rather than scientific and historical arguments made to legitimize it.

Religious Authority

From the time of Jesus, religious authority had more to do with personal authority than with biblical authority. Jesus gave authority to his disciples, and in the early church, the disciples represented God's primary religious authority. Later, the book of Acts talks about how the council of Jerusalem spoke authoritatively on behalf of the church, and that it was no longer the disciples who gave leadership, but the elder James (Acts 15:1-21). Appeals to Scripture (mostly the Old Testament) were made, but primary authority resided in the church leadership.

For centuries thereafter, religious authority was primarily exercised by church leadership, and in Western Christianity, the

Pope and magisterial traditions established by the Catholic Church in Rome in due course became the primary religious authorities. Again, in Western Christianity, Protestant Reformers such as Luther thought that the leadership of the Catholic Church had become corrupt, and so the only authority to which Christians could reliably default was Scripture. *Sola Scriptura* (Lat., 'Scripture alone') became a slogan of the Reformation as Protestants needed to establish their alternative churches, especially in Continental Europe where Luther oversaw schism from the Catholic Church.

Reformation also took place in Britain, but leadership in the Church of England (also known as Anglicanism) wanted to steer a *via media* (Lat., 'middle way') between Catholicism and Continental Protestantism. In steering this middle way, Anglican theologians admitted that Christians rely on more authorities than just Scripture. We also rely on reason and tradition. In later Protestant revivals, experience was increasingly thought to serve authoritatively in how one understood Christian beliefs, values, and practices. For example, Wesley appealed to experience as a genuine — albeit secondary — religious authority, which included personal religious experience (e.g., conversion, prayer) along with other scientific and historical experiences. He did not consider himself to be innovative theologically, but rather acknowledge how all Christians and churches did theology, within the context of Scripture, tradition, reason, and experience.

Scripture, Tradition, Reason, and Experience

There are many ways that Christians refer to the contextual nature of their beliefs, values, and practices, and the Wesleyan quadrilateral is only one way of doing so. But there needs to be some awareness of the interdependent relationship between multiple authorities that affect how Christians and churches realistically function. Although Scripture may be believed to hold a place of priority as divine revelation, Scripture was revealed in particular historical and literary contexts, being written in various genres. So, we need to acknowledge the dynamic interconnectedness that occurs between Scripture, tradition, reason, and experience, at least, in understanding how Christians and churches actually go about deciding and applying their beliefs and values.

From time to time in church history, Christians have reduced theology to only one mode of reflection, elevating Scripture, reason, tradition, or experience above all other modes of thinking about God. For example, deists in the eighteenth century made reason primary over Scripture and tradition, and liberal Protestants in the 19th century made experience primary over all other religious authorities. These theologies jeopardized historic understandings of Scripture and orthodox Christian tradition, though their influence continues.

In our so called postmodern era, Christians have less confidence in the reliability of any religious authority, including biblical authority. Although they may believe that God transcends such limitations, people do not transcend them, and so Christian beliefs, values, and practices must be seen as contingent, rather than as certain knowledge. They are influenced by the particular socio-cultural context in which they arose. Scripture too must be regarded as being contingent—to some degree—by the particular situations in which it arose. Neither rational argumentation nor empirical evidence can be seen to legitimize Christian claims to truth; they are faith claims, rather than claims legitimized by rational or empirical argumentation. And while it may seem like a leap of faith to believe in the Bible, even the Bible itself explains that this is often the case. As the Apostle Paul noted, "we walk by faith, not by sight" (2 Cor 5:7).

Interpretation of Scripture

Given what we have learned about the situated nature of Scripture, how should it be interpreted? In the early church, Christians were acutely aware of the difficulty in interpreting biblical passages. Two early forms of interpretation were known as literal and allegorical (or figurative, symbolic) interpretations. However, Christians knew that sometimes a literal interpretation isn't always the best way to interpret a biblical passage. For example, what do we do with passages that suggest that you gouge out your eyes or cut off your hands if they contribute to sinfulness (e.g., Matthew 5:29, 18:9), when such practices are not reported in Scripture, nor in church history? What do we do with passages that exhort greeting one another with a "holy kiss" or prohibiting women from wearing "gold, pearls, or expensive clothes," when such practices are usually considered culturally relative (e.g., Romans 16:16; 1 Timothy 2:9)? Sometimes passages difficult to understand were thought to be better interpreted by an allegorical approach that includes explanations that make use of analogies, metaphors, typologies, or other symbolic imagery. In the early church, allegorical interpretations were often thought to supersede literal interpretations, including literal interpretations of Genesis and Revelation.

Most Christians tried to be inductive in their biblical interpretation. They wanted biblical texts to speak for themselves, rather than drawing heavily on theological resources and church traditions. Induction emphasizes the firsthand study of biblical texts, using Scripture to interpret Scripture, Often times Christians will jump immediately to dictionaries, commentaries, and other resources readily available today, especially online resources. While these can be very helpful, we also need to remember that the Bible has ample meaning on its own. People would do well today to study inductively Scripture for themselves, before reaching conclusions about biblical texts that they then preach, teach, or bear witness about deductively. Both induction and deduction are important for communicating the gospel, especially as found in Scripture, but starting inductively helps aid people in learning about biblical text for themselves.

In time, other forms or interpretation or biblical criticism arose. It would take too long to talk about all of them. Suffice it to say that, at least, three things need to be considered when interpreting Scripture. First, the genre of a biblical text needs to be considered. Is the text historical narrative, or is it a parable, which should be interpreted differently? Other genres include psalms, hymns, poetry, epistles, apocalyptic literature, and more, which require different approaches to interpreting Scripture.

Second, study the historical context of the biblical text. What was going at the time of the writing? What was going on elsewhere throughout the ancient Near East that may have relevance to the interpretation of Scripture? Historical, archaeological, and other behavioral scientific information can greatly benefit the interpretation of a particular biblical text.

Third, study the literary context of the biblical text, for example, in relationship to other writings that occurred near the time that Scripture was written. Too often Christians have projected on biblical texts what they want to say, and not what Scripture says. This projection is known as 'eisegesis' (the projecting of an interpretation upon a text), rather than 'exegesis' (the critical interpretation of a text). Christians do not always want to study, at length, the literary context of a text. Yet, understanding the context of biblical passages is crucial when it comes to interpreting adequately what Scripture has to say, rather than what its interpreters may want it to say. As D.A. Carson has said: "A text without a context is a pretext for a proof text."

Final Comments

Our modern terminology, theology, and apologetics are not needed to defend the sufficiency of Scripture; God's grace is sufficient. The affirmation of sufficiency does not preclude the historical and critical study of Scripture, but it humbly admits the need to utilize more, including the use of church history, logical thinking, and relevant experience.

Most Christians retain belief in the primacy of biblical authority, but nowadays affirm it with a more contextual and thus relevant understanding of its application to people — spiritually and physically, individually and collectively, temporally and eternally. As such, Scripture remains the principal authority by which Christians decide their beliefs, values, and practices.

Part Five

"So That Everyone Who Believes May Not Perish"

Our Choices Make a Difference

One of my favorite hobbies is gardening. When I was a kid, gardening—especially pulling weeds—was a chore I detested. However, as an adult, I find weeding, pruning, planting fruit and vegetables, and growing flowers to be invigorating. I like to get down on my knees, sift my hands through dirt, and water newly embedded plants. It's a creative outlet as well as a physically refreshing task. Gardening helps me to relax, think, and enjoy natural beauty.

Gardening, farming, and shepherding were common analogies used in Scripture for talking about the workings of God in the lives of people. Jesus said, "I am the vine, you are the branches" (John 15:5). Elsewhere, Jesus said, "I am the good shepherd. The good shepherd lays down his life for the sheep" (John 10:11). Similar analogies appear in Scripture that communicate how God works in and through the lives of people.

How plants and animals grew were generally a mystery to biblical writers, which contributed to their amazement about God's creation and about God's providential care for it. Scripture talks about how people learned more and more over time about agriculture and animal husbandry. Over the centuries, people have learned far more about gardening, farming, and shepherding. And yet, there remains a sense of wonder every time a plant sprouts out of the ground, or a baby sheep is birthed. It's as if wondrous powers are at work, which we can never fully comprehend. Perhaps we are reminded of the sovereignty of God, not only over nature, but also over our lives, and over our salvation.

There are Christian theologies that emphasize the sovereignty of God, and how God determines effectually the lives of people, including the election of some to salvation (and perhaps also the reprobation of others to damnation). But overwhelmingly in church history, Christians have believed that God works by grace in people's lives in order that they might respond to the promptings of God's Holy Spirit, drawing them into cooperation with the grace

123

of God to accept or reject God's workings, including that of salvation.

Although it seems pious to say that "God did everything," and that "we did nothing," the reality is that we think, say, and do things, for which God holds us accountable. How is this possible? The apostle Paul gives a farming analogy about human responsibility in 1 Corinthians 3:6, where he talks about God's role and people's role regarding spiritual matters; he said: "I planted, Apollos [another disciple] watered, but God gave the growth." It is only by divine grace that spiritual increase occurs, but as the analogy states, God still expects people to "plant" and "water." So, to what degree are people thought responsible for planting and watering in ways that contribute to their salvation, as well as for how they are to live the Christian in life?

In Scripture, the responsibility people have is best understood in terms of the various covenants, or promises, that God made. Although there are different ways that God's covenants with people may be understood, since each one was uniquely made between God and individuals (and groups of individuals), some responsibility for obedience on behalf of people to the covenants was expected by God. Failure to abide by the covenants resulted in sin; success in abiding by them represented righteous, just living. As such, some degree of freedom of choice was thought to exist. Otherwise, how could God justly hold people accountable for their decision-making?

Early Christian Debate

Early Christian debate about people's role, especially with regard to salvation, began with Augustine's theological diatribe against the bishop Pelagius in the fourth century. Although we know little directly about Pelagius' writings, Augustine accused the bishop of advocating works-righteousness by which people earn or merit their salvation from God. In Scripture, the apostle Paul clearly rejected works-righteousness (e.g., Ephesians 2:8-9).

Instead Augustine argued that people suffer from original sin and can do nothing to earn or merit their salvation. People must rely totally upon God and God's predestination for salvation. God's predestination occurred before the creation of the world, and in this life, the faith that we have indicates that we are elect; otherwise, we would not have faith (e.g., Ephesians 4:1). From Augustine's perspective, divine grace is effectual (or irresistible), and so those who have faith should give thanks and praise to God, since there are no conditions that people must fulfill for their gift of salvation.

Augustine may well be the most influential theologian in church history, and yet this was one area where the majority of Christians disagreed with him. Instead, Caesarius of Arles and others in the early church believed that God gives people a measure of freedom, which is initiated, enabled, and completed by divine grace, but genuinely free nonetheless, undetermined by external causes. God self-restricts power over people in order that they may have freedom to accept or reject the things of God. Caesarius eminently presided over the Council of Orange in 425, which included Canon 25:

> This also do we believe, in accordance with the Catholic faith, that after grace received through baptism, all the baptized are able and ought, with the aid and co-operation of Christ, to fulfil all duties needful for salvation, provided they are willing to labour faithfully. But that some men have been predestinated to evil by divine power, we not only do not believe, but if there be those who are willing to believe so evil a thing, we say to them with all abhorrence anathema.

"Anatehma," the word that Caesarius uses to describe followers of predestination, is one of the greatest possible insults that anyone could have spoken in the 5th century. Most Christians thereafter affirmed that people are to cooperate with God, both for their salvation and for Christian living. Such cooperation is not responsible for the divine "increase," so to speak, but it did describe some of the conditional "planting" and "watering" expected of them by God (cf. 1 Corinthians 3:6).

Augustinianism and Semi-Augustinianism

The view advocated by Caesarius has sometimes been referred to as *Semi-Augustinianism*, since it still emphasizes that salvation is indeed a divine gift, which people receive at the initiation of God. But that does not preclude genuine responsibility on the part of people to accept or to reject salvation. Moreover, the Christian life is to be understood as an ongoing relationship between believers and God's Holy Spirit, partnering in ways that tangibly demonstrate believers' love for God as well as love for themselves and others. So, our choices make a difference in many ways. Examples of Christians and churches who affirm Semi-Augustinianism include Catholics, Orthodox Churches, Anglicans, Arminians, Methodists, Pentecostals, and others. They overwhelmingly make up the majority of Christians, both past and present.

To be sure, a measure of mystery permeates the relationship between God's role and people's role in the matters of life. And it isn't just God and people that have the ability to impact the world. Nature itself has a measure of independence, created by God, which can be a hindrance to people as much as a help. In this context, there is no such thing as unlimited freedom. On the contrary, people are always limited in many ways. For example, how can people ever know for sure about the extent of freedom that they have? How extensively does their personal, biological, and socio-cultural context affect their decision-making? As one might expect, human freedom represents a faith affirmation that Christians have, which they believe is articulated in Scripture and corroborated by experience. Despite the natural and supernatural (including demonic) influences that challenge human decision-making, it is believed that people have sufficient freedom — and responsibility — to do that which God wants them to do, which is both enabled and aided by the Holy Spirit.

During the Protestant Reformation, Augustinianism made a comeback in the theology of Luther and Calvin. They thought that God is sovereign, and that the totally depraved state of humanity precluded any human condition for salvation. Calvin went further, arguing that God predetermined both who would be saved and who would be damned. Followers of Calvin sometimes call this double predestination, since people's eternal well-being — both salvation and damnation — depend upon God's decrees before the creation of the world, rather than upon the condition of people's choices. Calvin said that people may be said to have freedom, of sorts, but it was freedom to do that which is compatible with divine predestination, since God's grace is irresistible.

Confused?

Christians today sometimes become confused by these debates, and understandably so. This is due, in part, to limited categories with which they think about the subject of human freedom. For example, if affirming the sovereignty of God represents one's highest belief, then any talk about people's role in decision-making may seem heretical! But this kind of either-or thinking is inadequate and naïve, both with regard to Scripture and to the ways that people actually live their lives. Again, it seems pious to say that God does everything, and that God meticulously plans all that occurs (even sin and evil, pain and suffering), but it is not sufficient in understanding Scripture and experience. Although some biblical references suggest that God meticulously controls and plans everything, more of Scripture suggest that God holds people accountable for their choices — with regard to sin, salvation, and the Christian life. The plans of God for humanity are more general, rather than meticulous; generally speaking, God created a context for people, conducive for responsible decision-making. Although God may sovereignly at any time intervene in the world and work miraculously, and God does this from time to time, God mostly works persuasively in the lives of people, calling for their responsible decision-making, rather than compellingly ordering every detail of their lives.

Indeed, most Christians affirm more of a Semi-Augustinian view of human free will (or, as Wesley preferred to say, "free grace"), since even people's free, uncoerced choices are enabled by God's grace working in their lives. Still, their choices make a difference! It is no wonder that Scripture puts so much emphasis upon people's choices, upon the need for them to repent, believe, and abide by covenants God made with them. In particular, the new covenant of the gospel talks about the need for people to choose wisely in relating with God, oneself, and others in ways that are righteous, just, and good.

Open Theism

In talking about human freedom, open theism represents a relative latecomer in discussions about God's role and people's role in the occurrences of life. During the twentieth century, some Christians came to believe more strongly in the freedom that people have, in part, because of their changing view of God. Open theists argue that a more faithful reading of Scripture reveals a depiction of God that most Christians in church history have overblown, giving

God more expansive attributes than biblical texts describe. For example, Scripture talks about God changing God's mind, regret (or repentance, depending on the biblical translation) over divine decisions made, and anger over people's actions. Indeed, the very act of prayer assumes that people may change God's mind or plans by their intercessions.

Although Open theists believe that God is all powerful and all knowing, they do not believe that God can know the unknowable, that is, that which has not yet occurred (i.e., the future; also known as counterfactuals). Thus, because God knows all that is knowable in the past and present, God can masterfully predict the future. But not even God knows for sure what will happen, regarding what people will decide, and what natural anomalies might occur.

This view of God is different from historic Christian understandings, and it helps to explain some problematic biblical passages, but not all of them. For example, if God does not know the future for certain, then how does one account for prophecy in Scripture? Although open theists may admit that they cannot explain the specificity of every biblical prophecy, they argue that most of them can be dismissed as having been made conditionally. For example, some were based upon people's obedience or disobedience to God's commands, or some refer to specific intentions that God had planned for the future. With regard to prayer, however, open theists argue that their theology makes the most sense of Scripture. People in Scripture, including people today, pray with the intention of changing present circumstances, or of changing God's mind or plans for their lives. Open theism is not unorthodox in the sense that past Christians never raised similar questions, and so it remains to be seen whether open theistic views will capture the allegiance of present day Christians and churches.

Final Comments

As a parent, I'm grateful that all three of my daughters have turned out all right, if I may say so myself! But I reserve the parental right still to be concerned about them. (And don't even begin to talk to me about worrying over grandchildren!) I do not control my children, and the older they become, the less control (and responsibility) I have over them. But I would like to think that my

parenting had some positive effects upon their decision-making —
past, present, and future.

The analogy of God as parent is a powerful way to think
about our relationship with God. Like a parent, especially with
younger children, God wants to nurture us in ways that we not only
become more responsible, but also become more humble in
responding to God in faith and repentance, so that we may receive
God's provision for eternal life in heaven. But the restoration of
relationship with God impacts how we live here and now, and not
only about the future. We ought not to be "so heavenly minded that
we are of no earthly good," as the saying goes. Instead we ought to
think about how our decisions make a difference, both with regard
to how God guides just, righteous, and loving decision-making
now, and how we may receive the full extent of God's benefits in
heaven.

Orders of Salvation

When I was young, I was enthralled by stories about dramatic conversion experiences: I learned about the apostle Paul, a former persecutor of Christians who was blinded by a flash of light and heard the voice of God before converting to Christianity. I learned about Augustine, who lived a life of lust before coming to terms with his evil deeds (including, most famously, his theft of pears). And I admired the conversion story of the famous Protestant reformer Luther, who confronted his faith amidst the flashes and torrents of a thunderstorm. Contemporary Christian celebrities also testify to having lived lives of drunken debauchery, drug experimentation, and wanton sex before converting, usually in an instantaneous moment of illumination, faith, and repentance, which was followed (seemingly) by uninterrupted stories of successful living.

Of course, in my youth, I may have romanticized these spiritual success stories, and to a certain extent I also resented them. Although I was a Christian, in my understanding of that term, I had a rather boring spiritual background. It mostly involved growing up in the church. How could I ever share my Christian testimony with others if I did not have a dramatic conversion story? (In addition, I secretly envied that others had had the chance to indulge in alcohol, drugs, and sex, and I'd missed out on the opportunity to do so.) In a sense, I felt cheated. Why did God give some people amazingly memorable spiritual experiences, while other Christians struggled over time with questions, doubts, or boring—relatively speaking—spiritual lives?

Although I attended a secular university, I read *The Varieties of Religious Experience* by William James. He did not speculate about the origin of religious experiences, but how they may be empirically studied and evaluated. Basically, James suggested that people's religious experiences may have as much (or more) to do with their personal and cultural backgrounds, than they have to do with God's involvement or design. I found this behavioral scientific concept

131

freeing, since it helped me to evaluate more sensibly my own religious experiences, as unpretentious as they seemed.

Throughout church history, people's accounts about how they became Christians reveal a remarkably wide spectrum of experiences. Although one may have grown up with (or been taught) a narrow understanding of religious conversion, people testify to a surprising variety of ways with regard to how they became Christians. This variety also appears in Scripture, though some verses tend to be emphasized more than others. Thus, we should not be surprised to find that a number of different "orders," or experiences of salvation have been talked about by Christians, both past and present.

Salvation in Scripture

What does Scripture have to say about salvation in general and conversion in particular? John 3:16 is a great place to start in exploring this question. It says:

> For God so loved the world that he gave his only Son, so that everyone who believes in him may not perish but may have eternal life.

It seems that, from the perspective of people — who are the subjects of salvation — the only condition is belief, or faith. Similar kinds of teaching can be found throughout Scripture.

However, other passages in Scripture suggest other so-called conditions for salvation. For example, at the beginning of the gospel of Mark, which is considered the first Gospel written, other conditions are mentioned:

> Jesus came to Galilee, proclaiming the good news of God, and saying, 'The time is fulfilled, and the kingdom of God has come near; repent, and believe in the good news' (Mark 1:14-15).

So, both repentance and belief are required conditions for salvation.

On the day of Pentecost, the largest evangelistic event in Scripture is reported, with more than 3,000 converts. Peter's call to salvation consisted of the following:

> Repent, and be baptized every one of you in the name of Jesus Christ so that your sins may be forgiven; and you will receive the gift of the Holy Spirit (Acts 2:38).

Here nothing is said about belief or faith; instead, Peter told people to repent and be baptized, and then they would receive the "gift of the Holy Spirit," that is, salvation. These biblical references cast

132

suspicion upon the Protestant Reformation slogan about salvation 'by faith alone' (Lat., *sola fide*). After all, Scripture does not explicitly say that people are saved (or justified before God) by faith alone, though it does say the opposite in James 2:24: "You see that a person is justified by works and not by faith alone."

Scripture does not prescribe any particular order of salvation. But it does describe a variety of ways that people genuinely converted, for example, by faith, repentance, baptism, and other means. Thus, caution must be used in thinking about any particular order of salvation (or experience of salvation) as normative for everyone. People ought to be free to become Christian in whatever way they experience it their particular context, whether it occur gradually or instantaneously, within the context of the church or outside it, or whether it occur individually or collectively. In Scripture, entire households converted and were baptized all at once (e.g., Acts 16:33), which should further humble us in terms of the particular ways by which we understand how people experience Christian salvation.

Orders of Salvation

After the Protestant Reformation, a variety of churches and groups of churches emerged. In order to distinguish between themselves, attention was sometimes given to differing orders of salvation that each promoted. These differences were theologically important, and helped people to see how the various Christian traditions understood and applied Scripture.

Prior to the Protestant Reformation, Catholic Churches largely understood the way to salvation through the sacraments. Catholics affirm seven sacraments, and five of them largely have to do with salvation and living the Christian life. First, the sacrament of Baptism cleanses people — including infants — of original sin, and makes them Christians, children of God, and heirs of eternal life. Second, the sacrament of Confirmation gives those who were baptized the opportunity to confirm the faith in which they were baptized, having reached an age of reason (or accountability), and to receive an increase of sanctifying grace, gifts, and spiritual strength. Third, the sacrament of Eucharist (or Holy Communion) graciously strengthens Christians and serves to unite the Catholic Church. Fourth, the sacrament of Reconciliation (or Penance) has to do with the pardoning of sins after baptism, emphasizing the need for continual faith and renewal in living the Christian life. Fifth, the sacrament of the Anointing of the Sick aids people who need healing, of one sort or another; it also aids people in their frailty as finite, sinful people, who await God's gift of eternal life. (Note: The other two Catholic sacraments will be discussed in a later chapter.)

Orthodox Christians have a similar view of the role of the sacraments for salvation. They differ in how they think about salvation in relationship to *theosis* (Gk., 'deification'), which represents an ongoing process of spiritual transformation by divine grace. By *theosis*, people are saved and progressively grow in Christlikeness, as they participate in God's Spirit, with whom Christians grow in spiritual union (or communion) with God.

Protestant Orders of Salvation

Protestant traditions distinguished themselves from other Protestants (as well as Catholics) by talking about their understanding of how people ordinarily become Christians. Although Christians from the same theological tradition may differ among themselves, the following orders of salvation provide a beginning point for conversation. (This list is not exhaustive of Protestant views.) The words in the following outline may seem a bit confusing or unfamiliar: Illumination? Regeneration? Glorification? What do these mean? I will explain these in greater detail further in this section.

Lutherans: calling, illumination, conversion (faith, repentance), regeneration, justification, sanctification, union with Christ, and glorification

Reformed (Calvinists): election, predestination, effectual calling, regeneration, faith, repentance, justification, sanctification, and glorification

Arminians: calling, faith, repentance, regeneration, justification, perseverance, and glorification

Wesleyans: calling, conversion (faith, repentance), regeneration, justification, assurance, repentance after justification and gradual sanctification, entire sanctification, and glorification

For those unfamiliar with the aforementioned terms, let me give general definitions for them, especially with regard to salvation:

Calling has to do with God's call for salvation (or service), and *effectual calling* has to do with God's call as being irresistible.

Illumination has to do with understanding God's call.

Predestination has to do with God's determination of who will be saved; some Christians consider predestination irresistibly decreed by God, while other Christians consider it based on God's foreknowledge of who will (or will not) believe.

Conversion has to do with a turning to God (faith) and turning from sin (repentance); some orders of salvation talk about conversion, while others talk about faith and repentance.

Faith has to do with trusting someone or something, and *repentance* has to do with sorrow over and confession of sin.

Regeneration has to do with the transformation of believers into greater righteousness (holiness, perfection), and along with regeneration, *justification* has to do with how God views people "as if" they have already become righteous, due to Jesus' atonement.

Perseverance has to do with being steadfast in the faith with which one converted.

Assurance has to do with God-given confidence of salvation, which is the privilege of believers.

Sanctification has to do with the ongoing regenerative process of transforming believers into greater righteousness; entire sanctification has to do with the belief that believers may experience a heightened degree of Christlikeness in this life, aided by *repentance after justification and gradual sanctification.*

Union with Christ is a variously understood term, which either has to do with a believer's intimate relationship with Jesus Christ, or a step in the effectual calling of a believer.

Glorification has to do with the reception of eternal life in heaven.

Extensive comparisons and contrasts may be made about the aforementioned orders of salvation. However, I will only focus upon one topic, namely, the role of divine grace. Is saving grace effectual (and irresistible), or is it prevenient (and resistible)?

Reformed (Calvinist) Christians are heavily invested in saying that salvation occurs effectually, based upon their belief in the eternal election and predestination of God. Stages of salvation are effectual, that is, irresistible: calling, regeneration, faith, repentance, justification, sanctification, and glorification. Salvation is God's task, and not the task of people. People act compatibly with God's effectual, irresistible grace, but there are no conditions—technically speaking—for which they are responsible in the order of salvation. Lutherans largely agreed with Reformed views about effectual grace and salvation, though they did not focus upon them quite as overpoweringly.

In contrast, Arminian and Wesleyan Christians put more emphasis upon how people are partners with God's Holy Spirit in bringing about personal salvation. This is what we mean when we talk about prevenient grace—a synergistic cooperation between individuals and God's Holy Spirit. God's Spirit works in ways that calls them, and persuades them to have faith and repentance, which are conditions for receiving God's free gift of eternal life. Likewise, after conversion, Christians must continue to exercise faith, hope, and love in order to maintain their reconciled relationship with God, since relationships must be maintained and nurtured. In this model salvation is a collaborative effort between God and human beings.

During the Protestant Reformation, Lutheran and Reformed Christians reaffirmed an Augustinian theological emphasis on the sovereignty of God and the irresistibility of God's provision of salvation. In contrast, Anglicans, Arminians, and Wesleyans reaffirmed a Semi-Augustinian theological emphasis on the prevenience of divine grace and the resistibility of God's provision of salvation, while maintaining belief in God's sovereignty. The latter believed that Lutheran and Reformed Christians went too far in rejecting people's role in salvation. Instead, Anglicans, Arminians, and Wesleyans agreed with historic Catholic and Orthodox churches that affirmed more of a Semi-Augustinian view of people cooperating with divine grace in choosing to accept God's provision of salvation.

Salvation: A Single, Complex Event

Some Christians have described salvation as a verb, rather than as a noun, since it is dynamic, relational, and in need of ongoing human participation. Indeed, the provision by God for salvation is a gift of divine grace, which Jesus provided for us, and it can never be achieved as a matter of human work or merit. In response, people are to decide—by God's grace—to accept or reject salvation. Since the restorative dimensions of salvation are ongoing, Christians do not cease from their participatory involvement post-conversion. On the contrary, they are to be actively involved with the sanctifying grace of God, which enhances their lives as well as their relations with others.

Salvation is not just a single event; it is a complex event that entails ongoing responsibilities for people's relationship with God, themselves, and with others. As C.S. Lewis said, Christianity is both 'easy' and 'hard.' It is easy because salvation is a gift. We ought never to forget that we are saved, not because we deserve it, but because we humbly turn to God for our forgiveness, since we fall far short of righteous and just living. On the other hand, Christianity is hard because God wants converts to commit their whole lives to God—all their values, expectations, and securities. Paul says:

> I appeal to you therefore, brothers and sisters, by the mercies of God, to present your bodies as a living sacrifice, holy and acceptable to God, which is your spiritual worship (Romans 12:1).

It is a hard sacrifice, but it is worth the risk. In the Gospel of Matthew Jesus invites people into salvation with the phrase

> Come to me, all you that are weary and are carrying heavy burdens, and I will give you rest. Take my yoke upon you... for my yoke is easy, and my burden is light" (Matthew 11:28-30).

Jesus uses the image of a yoke, which is the instrument that lies across the backs of livestock as they carry forward a load, such as plowing farmland. Jesus says that the yoke is easy and the burden is light—but we have to remember that it is still a yoke, and we share some responsibility in pulling our salvation forward. I have always liked how the missionary Jim Elliot described what it is like to follow Jesus: "He is no fool who gives what he cannot keep to gain what he cannot lose." We have more to gain from salvation than we have to lose, but that doesn't mean that there isn't sacrifice involved.

So, salvation has to do with more than getting a "get out of hell free card" or "free ticket to heaven," though there is an element of truth to both clichés. Salvation represents a starting-point into new relationship with God, a relationship that relishes in forgiveness, restoration, and the promise of eternal life. Salvation also represents a starting-point, in this lifetime, of an ongoing relationship with God through the Holy Spirit.

The Holy Spirit is not content to let you bide your time until you die. God wants to work in and through your lives, helping Christians to become and act more like Jesus. Then they may be more loving toward God, themselves, and others. Indeed, God wants to minister in abundant ways through Christians and churches. They do not receive 'cheap grace,' as Dietrich Bonhoeffer admonished. Salvation was bought with a price, the price of Jesus' atoning life, death, and resurrection. In thanks and praise to God, Christians ought to open themselves to the dynamic ways in which the Holy Spirit leads them in Christ-like living.

Final Comments

There is no prescribed order of salvation, not even in Scripture. God welcomes everyone to be restored from lives of sin, rebelliousness, indifference, and other hindrances to a right relationship with God. Do not get hung up on particular views of becoming, or of being a Christian. It is a waste of time and worrisome energy!

I think God welcomes as many who desire, in as many ways as are necessary, for people to return to God's loving embrace. People need to take a crucial step towards salvation, regardless of whether it happens during the rites and rituals of confirmation, dramatic conversion at a revival meeting, or quiet acceptance while reading a book. All are welcome!

Justice and Justification

While attending seminary, I met a fellow student who spent a weekend in Washington, DC, with other seminarians, protesting against The Tax Equity and Fiscal Responsibility Act (TEFRA) of 1982. For all of President Ronald Reagan's talk about tax cutting, TEFRA was the largest peacetime tax increase in U.S. history. So, seminarians traveled to protest against political policies that disproportionately raised taxes for the middle and lower classes, while preserving exorbitant tax cuts for the upper class.

When my friend returned, I asked her about her experience. She told me about how the protestors considered it part of their moral obligation as Christians to advocate on behalf of all that impoverishes people — physically, economically, and politically as well as spiritually, both in and outside of the church. My friend told me about the prayers prayed, hymns sung, signs displayed, protest routes marched, and sermons and speeches proclaimed. Admittedly, it was a world of activism unfamiliar to me. I had briefly protested at the university that I attended, advocating for its divestment from multinational corporations that supported apartheid in South Africa. But I had been a reticent protester, and had given lackluster support to the cause.

Then my friend shocked me by saying that, during the protest, she had never felt closer to God in her entire life. This statement floored me! I came from a religious background that found closeness with God by partaking in the sacraments, studying Scripture, praying, fasting, or holy living. But closeness with God in civil protest? That did not compute in my mind or experience. Yet, over the years, since the conversation with my friend, I have come to appreciate that there are many ways that people feel close with God. Why shouldn't that sense of spiritual intimacy occur in the midst of advocating in ways that are righteous and just?

Throughout church history, Christians and churches have variously involved themselves with matters of justice. More often than not, Christians preferred to talk about justification, rather than justice. Justification has to do with how God looks upon converts "as if" they are just, or as if they are righteous, because of Jesus' atonement on their behalf. Christians like to talk about justification, since it involves their eternal well-being! Justice, on the other hand, has to do with fairness, equity, impartiality, and respect for people. Christians haven't talked as much about justice. Why? There's no single answer to this question, of course. Yet, justice and justification are related to one another. Moreover, both are important in Scripture, and so both should be promoted and not neglected.

Translating *Dikaiosuné*

The Greek word *dikaiosuné* in the New Testament may be translated as either "righteousness" or "justice." In most translations, the word righteousness is used, rather than justice, but why? Consider, for example, Jesus' beatitude in the Sermon on the Mount: "Blessed are those who hunger and thirst for *righteousness*, for they will be filled" (Matthew 5:6). But what if it was translated: "Blessed are those who hunger and thirst for *justice*"? The meaning would be quite different! In fact, given the context of Jesus' beatitudes, using the word justice makes more sense than righteousness. Consider a later beatitude: "Blessed are those who are persecuted for righteousness' sake, for theirs is the kingdom of heaven" (Matthew 5:10). Although people may persecute Jesus' followers for being righteous, it is more likely—in context—that they would be persecuted for advocating justice. Subsequent verses in Jesus' Sermon on the Mount talk about other ways that his followers are to confront injustice through non-violent, civil disobedience, for example, by 'turning the other cheek' or 'going the extra mile' (Matthew 5:38-41).

Justice is a prominent theme throughout the Old Testament. God is described as a God of justice, and those who follow God are expected to act justly as well. Micah 6:8 famously talks about the priority of promoting justice:

> He has told you, O mortal, what is good; and what does the Lord require of you but to do justice, and to love kindness, and to walk humbly with your God?"

Many other verses could be quoted to talk about how justice should be actively promoted: first, in relations with people one-on-one, and second, collectively in relationship with people both inside and outside one's community, tribe, or nation.

Justice in the Old Testament differed from justice in ancient Rome. Romans emphasized distributive justice, or justice of equality (Lat., *iustitia distributiva*), which connotes equivalence without respect of person. Romans were well known for their emphasis on justice, law, and equity for Roman citizens. In the Old Testament, justice included restoration between God and people (and between people and people), advocacy against societal as well as interpersonal injustices, and the distribution of goods for those suffering in society from poverty, sickness, or neglect. Ancient Israelites were also known for their emphasis on justice, but their justice, laws, and equity were intended to extend beyond Israel. For example, they were to welcome foreigners (strangers, aliens), and treat them equally, since the Israelites had once been foreigners in Egypt (Leviticus 19:34; Deuteronomy 10:19). Although God revealed to Moses commandments and codes for the Israelites to obey, they were intended for all, and not just for Israelite citizenry.

Part of the problem in failing to recognize the importance of justice in the New Testament may perhaps be nominal, that is, a matter of words chosen for biblical translations and for Christian discourse. But words make a difference, and Christians ought to be aware of translation challenges. Let us look, for example, at translating the Greek word *koinonia* into the English translation. Usually the word is translated as "fellowship." But *koinonia* can also be translated as "sharing," "participation," or "contribution." At times, Scripture translations have used multiple words for *koinonia*, such as "fellowship *and* sharing" (emphasis mine), which may convey meaning better than an attempted word-for-word translation. After all, *koinonia* had to do with more than mere fellowship within one's tribe; it also had to do with tangibly sharing one's possessions with others. Perhaps the same could be said for *dikaiosuné*, which may be better translated as "justice *and* righteousness" (emphasis mine).

In the Old Testament, the prophets often paired both "justice" and "righteousness." The Book of Amos, for example, pairs the two, usually talking about justice first (Amos 5:7, 5:24, 6:12). Of course, Amos spoke in the Hebrew language, using the words *mišpāṭ* (justice) and *ṣәḏāqāh* (righteousness). In Amos 5:24, the prophet famously said: "But let justice roll down like waters, and righteousness like an ever-flowing stream." To Amos, God clearly wants socio-economic justice, in addition to pious righteousness. The two are not incompatible; nor can the two be separated.

Sometimes people contrast the Old and New Testaments, saying that the Old Testament deals with justice and righteousness, while the New Testament deals with grace and mercy. But is this the case? In some respects, the New Testament's demand for justice is stronger. No better example of this can be found than in Jesus.

Jesus' Ministry Self-Defined

How would you define Jesus' ministry? When appearing before people from his hometown of Nazareth, early in his ministry, Jesus was asked to read from the Hebrew Scriptures in the synagogue. Jesus chose the following Scriptures, based upon the account in Luke 4:17-21:

> He unrolled the scroll and found the place where it was written:"The Spirit of the Lord is upon me, because he has anointed me to bring good news to the poor. He has sent me to proclaim release to the captives and recovery of sight to the blind, to let the oppressed go free, to proclaim the year of the Lord's favour."
>
> And he rolled up the scroll, gave it back to the attendant, and sat down. The eyes of all in the synagogue were fixed on him. Then he began to say to them, "Today this Scripture has been fulfilled in your hearing."

In claiming to fulfill of Scripture, Jesus announced to all who would listen the kind of ministry he intended. But it was not a spiritualized ministry! It was a balanced ministry that, of course, involved care for the spiritual well-being of people through his proclamation of the "good news." However, Jesus did not merely preach and teach; he wanted to make sure that the poor were not excluded from the good news. Moreover, Jesus' ministry extended to those who are "captives...blind...[and] oppressed." If the aforementioned people, and others like them, are not attended to, then the followers of Jesus neglect being Christ-like in how they live and minister.

Jesus continued to perplex and then infuriate people in his hometown synagogue. In Luke 4:22, it says that the people, initially, were "amazed." But Jesus persisted, talking about how prophets were not accepted in their hometown. Examples that Jesus gave included (1) how Elijah had only been accepted by a woman from Sidon, who was a woman, and not a man, and also a foreigner with a different religious background (1 Kings 17:8-16), and (2) how Elisha only healed Naaman, a Syrian, also a foreigner with a different religious background (2 Kings 5:1-16). Then "all in the synagogue were filled with rage," and tried to kill Jesus (Luke 4:28-30, esp. 28). Scripture does not precisely say why they became enraged, but certainly Jesus had transgressed many lines: religious, ethnic, cultural, linguistic, and religious. Jesus was often counter-cultural in his life and ministry, which is surprising, since nowadays Christians and churches seem to be more invested in maintaining the status quo of society, rather than in living and ministering counter-culturally. For all the talk some Christians make about 'culture wars,' the warring has more to do with maintaining their privileged status as Christians, than with seeking justice, equitable civil rights, and compensation for those victimized in our contemporary culture.

Justification Implies Justice

Justification and justice are complementary in Scripture. It is not an either/or relationship, but a both/and relationship. Although some Christians might argue that matters of justice are a distraction to proclaiming justification, Scripture says that they are both important to Jesus and to the gospel. Salvation does not end with justification, that is, with the gift of God through Jesus, by which God forgives people's sins, and now treats them 'as if' they are holy, because of Jesus' atoning work on their behalf. On the contrary, converts are also called to be Christ-followers, in both word and deed. This following of Jesus implies care for those who are hungry, thirsty, ill-clothed, strangers, and in prison, as well as care for people's eternal well-being (see Matthew 25:31-46).

Sometimes Christians have theologies that say this physical, political, and economic world cannot be saved; only God can save it. They may even say that, based upon their expectations about the so-called "end-times" (from the Greek *eschaton*), they expect that the world will only get worse, before it gets better, and so why even try to make it better? But what if the world does get worse? Does that exempt Christians from living and advocating for righteousness?

From justice, including distributive justice on behalf of those in need? From loving their neighbors as themselves? No! The command to love God and our neighbors as ourselves means that we are called seek justice for others, just as we would for ourselves. This so-called Golden Rule implies equitable and just treatment among all people, and Jesus was quick to add that love for one's neighbor is not just for one's friends (community, tribe, or nation), but for everyone, including one's enemies (see Matthew 5:43-48).

Compassion and Advocacy

Christians have long been recognized for acts of compassion with regard to those who suffer from poverty, illness, homelessness, and other corporeal challenges. In this regard, they ministered to the *symptoms* of impoverishment. But what of the *causes* of impoverishment? It does not seem to care sufficiently for people if only the symptoms of impoverishment are treated, and not the causes as well. This requires advocacy on behalf of collective, societal, and political causes that lead to the unjust treatment of people. Such injustices can lead to the neglect or marginalization of vulnerable people, due to their racial background, ethnicity, gender, age, ability, language, nationality, sexual orientation, or religious background. Should Christians be concerned about such so-called social injustices? Well, Christians in Scripture were concerned about them!

For example, in Acts 6, complaints arose among members of the early church because Hellenist widows were being neglected in the distribution of food, whereas the Hebrew widows were fed. Probably, all were Jews, but the Hellenist widows were from a minority ethnic and possibly racial group; they also probably had different linguistic, cultural, and possibly national backgrounds. The twelve disciples responded immediately to this injustice by establishing deacons — a role within the church that is dedicated to serving those outside as well as inside one's own community. Usually, Christians and preachers I have heard talk about creation of the deaconate as a bureaucratic oversight, but I think it profoundly talks about how the early church responded to injustices that occurred to those who are different — who are "other."

Today Christians and churches ought to become more attentive to and activist on behalf of challenging injustices in today's society, locally and globally, since Christianity is not limited to one's family, church, tribe, or nation. After all, social problems are not limited to neglect and marginalization; they can also lead to discrimination, oppression, and violence. Churches can be just as guilty of injustice as can individuals. So, Christians ought not to conform to their particular socio-economic and political tribe, but be as empathetic and activist as was Jesus and the disciples in the early church.

Final Comments

Too often I have heard Christians say that there is not enough time, energy, and divine grace to be concerned about matters of justice and injustice; Christians only have time for justification, converting as many as possible before Jesus comes again. What a morally 'cheap grace'-oriented Christianity! It is no wonder that non-Christians recurrently berate Christians for their hypocrisy, exclusivity, and discrimination. But spiritually reductionist Christians do not represent the Jesus of Scripture; instead, they probably represent more about their personal, socio-economic, or political allegiances.

In Scripture, justice and justification are not an either/or matter. Jesus was concerned about justice as well as justification. With regard to justice, he cared for the poor as well as for the poor in spirit. Jesus healed those who suffered from physical illness as well as from soul-sickness. Jesus helped free people from unjust socio-economic bondage as well as from demonic bondage, for example, as when he cleansed the Jewish temple from moneychangers. Finally, he advocated for the just treatment of those who deserve punishment—both physical (breakers of civil law) and spiritual (breakers of God's law).

Varieties of Christian Spirituality

During the 1990s, my seminary colleagues and I read together an anthology that contained devotional writings from historic leaders in Christian spirituality. For each reading, a brief biography was given for the authors. I noticed that most of them were either unmarried, or else they wrote their devotional writings before or after they were married, usually by being widowed. According to my calculations, ninety-three percent of the so-called spiritual giants were unmarried and without little children as they wrote about how Christians ought to spend hours daily in reading, prayer, meditation, contemplation, and other spiritual disciplines. But how could I do this? In addition to teaching full-time, I was a single parent with three daughters under the age of ten. My schedule was incredibly full, and the prospect of setting aside multiple hours every day for spiritual formation was daunting, if not impossible.

At about the same time, I began teaching courses in Christian spirituality. Although my classes were more historical and theological than practical in orientation, I loved the subject matter. I appreciated the devotional literature available, and I learned — among other things — that there exists a variety of Christian spiritualities. Two in particular caught my attention. One was a family spirituality, which stated that during parental seasons of one's life, a primary way that one may be spiritual occurs through the care-giving and nurturing that one provides for children or other dependents, including those who are elderly or whose abilities are challenged in some way. Although I still prayed, read Scripture, attended church, and participated in other spiritual disciplines, my main way of sensing closeness with God occurred through care-giving for my family.

A second type to Christian spirituality that caught my attention was called studious spirituality. Authors who described this spirituality thought of it primarily as the study of Scripture, but it included other kinds of study. This type of studious spirituality was liberating to me, who had spent much of his life studying

Scripture, church history, theology, and other Christian writings. It is not as if I got out of doing other kinds of spiritual practices, exercises, or disciplines, but it helped me to focus on what I considered to be the most natural way for me to grow in faith, hope, and love.

Sometimes Christians feel defeated spiritually because they try to live up to the rigors of a particular (and, perhaps narrow) understanding of what it means to be spiritual, holy, perfect, godly, or Christ-like. Yet they may be unaware of the varieties of ways that Scripture talks about spiritual flourishing, and even more ways that later Christians developed as means of grace by which they believe the Holy Spirit works in and through their lives by sanctifying them into greater Christ-likeness. In this chapter, I want to talk about some of the many ways that Christians believe they may be faithful, obedient, and grow in grace, which in turn enables them to be more loving toward God and others—spiritually and physically, individually and collectively.

How Do We Grow Spiritually?

Like salvation, spiritual growth is due to God's grace, rather than to any work or merit of Christians. But that does not mean Christians do nothing toward their spiritual maturing. God gives people a measure of responsibility, aided by divine grace, by which they may choose (or not choose) to partner with the Holy Spirit for formation into greater Christ-likeness.

Some Christians believe that spiritual growth occurs entirely by God's initiative, and that God's plans for their formation into greater Christ-likeness is unplannable and irresistible. For them, the way Christians talk about spiritual growth and spiritual disciplines is too great of a risk, tempting Christians into thinking that they are not saved by grace through faith, as a gift of God. Instead, they argue, Christians should spend their time getting used to how both their salvation and spiritual maturation are unconditionally bestowed upon them.

But most Christians believe that God's Spirit works in and through their lives, and that there are general means (or channels, ways) of grace mentioned in Scripture by which they may partner with God in their spiritual formation. The means of grace that I'm talking about are not specific to a particular religious tradition (such as the sacraments in Catholicism). Rather, I am talking about a variety of spiritual practices, exercises, or disciplines mentioned in the Bible that can be useful for developing personal spirituality, regardless of your specific Christian denomination. These means of grace represent ways by which Christians have "planted" and "watered" for the spiritual "increase" that God supplies (1 Corinthians 3:6).

Examples of Spiritual Formation

Let me begin by making some general comments about the kinds of spiritual practices, exercises, and disciplines that Christians follow for the sake of their formation in Christlikeness. There is no consensus among Christians about how they best ought to live in order to partner with God's Holy Spirit in their spiritual formation. But I have always liked the directional analogy, used by Christians, that talks about how such practices aid in people's *upward* relationship with God, *inward* relationship with themselves, and *outward* relationship with others. These directions have been reflected in the devotional writings of Christians for centuries.

Dallas Willard talked a great deal about spiritual disciplines, and he provided a useful typology of them. Willard distinguished between spiritual disciplines of *abstinence* and spiritual disciplines of *engagement*. Spiritual disciplines of abstinence include the following: solitude, silence, meditation, contemplation, fasting, frugality, chastity, secrecy (or discretion), and sacrifice. Spiritual disciplines of engagement include the following: study, worship, celebration, service, prayer, fellowship, confession, and submission. In my experience, Christians in the Western part of the world are drawn far more to the disciplines of engagement, since they like to know what "more" they must do in order to cooperate with God's Holy Spirit—more activity, for example, for the sake of prayer and study. However, what Christians sometimes need is not more, but "less"—less activity, for example, for the sake of solitude and silence. They may need to slow down the busyness of their lives and spend more time being less busy in solitude and silence, if they want to experience greater intimacy (or communion) with God.

The number of spiritual practices, exercises, and disciplines is open-ended. There are spiritual practices explicitly described in Scripture, and there are spiritual practices inspired by Scripture that

Christians have practiced for centuries. Today, Christians are fashioning new means of grace by which to grow spiritually. For example, Adele Ahlberg Calhoun creatively talks about dozens of spiritual disciplines— both old and new—which she groups in seven categories: (1) Worship, (2) Open Myself to God, (3) Relinquish False Self, (4) Share My Life with Others, (5) Hear God's Words, (6) Incarnate the Life of Christ, and (7) Pray. Traditional spiritual disciplines she discusses include the Rule for Life, Examen, Iconography, Pilgrimage, and *Lectio Divina*. The Rule for Life has to do with developing habits or routines of spiritual practices. The Examen has to do with the daily discernment of God's role in the activities of one's life. Iconography has to do visualizing images of Christian saints and biblical characters to aid in worshiping God. Pilgrimage has to do with visiting holy sites for promoting prayerful attentiveness to God. *Lectio Divina* (Lat., "devotional reading") has to do with listening to God's voice as one meditatively reads Scripture.

Calhoun discusses many types of Christian prayer. *Prayer* has to do with talking with God, talking to God, and listening to God. It may occur individually or collectively, spoken or silent, liturgical or extemporaneous, kneeling or with hands raised. Here are a few well-known types of prayer: Adoration, Confession, Supplication (or Intercession), and Thanksgiving. Adoration has to do with giving praise and thanks for who God is. Confession has to do with sorrowfully confessing our faults and weaknesses to God, who forgives us. Supplication has to do with petitioning God on behalf of our concerns and worries, which includes prayerfully interceding on behalf of the needs of others. Thanksgiving has to do with thanking God, which includes thanks for our salvation and for the daily ways that God helps us.

Calhoun also discusses prayers that may not be as familiar to people, including Christians. They include Breath Prayer, Centering Prayer, Fixed-Hour Prayer, Labyrinth Prayer, Liturgical Prayer, and Prayer of Recollection. Breath prayer is a form of contemplative prayer that has to do with praying while breathing in, and praying while breathing out. Centering prayer is also a form of contemplative prayer that helps one center on the presence of Jesus Christ. Fixed-Hour Prayer has to do with predetermined times of prayer throughout the day; some church traditions follow a fixed

Liturgy of the Hours. Labyrinth Prayer has to do with following a simple marked path that aids one's contemplation of God. Liturgical Prayer has to do with a written or memorized prayer used for public or private devotion. Prayer of Recollection has to do with recalling the presence of God in the hubbub of everyday life, and thus resting in God. In sum, there are many ways to pray, and there is no limit to how one prayerfully meets God.

Just as there are many ways to pray, there are many ways that Christians undergo spiritual formation. Prayer represents, perhaps, the most common way they pursue intimacy with God, growth in Christlikeness, and express love toward God and others in ways that are tangible, just, and redemptive. Keep in mind that God causes spiritual formation to occur. Thus, there is no limit to the ways that spiritual formation takes place.

Traditions of Christian Spirituality

Over time different churches have emphasized different kinds of spirituality. You could say that each church or denomination has its unique spirituality, just as humans have unique personalities. You may recognize some of these traditions in your own experience, or at least, have come into contact with them.

First, evangelical churches emphasize evangelization, church planting, and missions. Their spiritual role model is the apostle Paul, and consider the Great Commission (Matthew 28:16-20) to be the standard for how Christians ought to be spiritual, namely, by proclaiming the gospel to others in word and deed.

Second, sacramental churches emphasize the role of the sacraments as special means of God's grace. They "celebrate" (or in other words, practice) the development of rites and rituals by first-century Christians in the book of Acts, especially the sacraments of Baptism and Eucharist (or Communion). For spiritual formation and ministry, they encourage public worship, liturgy, and other ceremonial practices developed in the epistles and historic churches — East and West, North and South.

Third, contemplative churches emphasize the spiritual disciplines, especially those that practice solitude, silence, and other exercises that lead to godliness, for example, Orthodox belief in *theosis* (Gk., 'deification'). In this tradition, Christians may utilize a short, repetitive prayer such as the Jesus Prayer: 'Lord Jesus Christ,

Son of God, have mercy on me, a sinner.' They may also utilize the threefold (1) purgative, (2) illuminative, and (3) unitive ways of spiritual formation. *Purgation* has to do with purging oneself of the cares and obligations of this world for the sake of contemplating God. *Illumination* has to do with divine insight God gives to contemplatives. *Union* has to do with intimate communion with God, considered the supreme relationship one may have with God in this life.

Fourth, studious churches emphasize the study, understanding, and application of Scripture. They promote Christian education, Scripture memorization, and the development of quality Christian literature. In addition to biblical and theological study aids, other types of Christian literature are produced, including novels, poetry, music, and other art forms.

Fifth, holiness churches emphasize the fruit of God's Holy Spirit, and how discipleship is essential for Christian living. Often accountability is emphasized in regular small group meetings, whether they be on Sunday mornings or mid-week, designed for the specific needs of people who attend. Such groups also help to organize effective ministries to people, inside and outside churches.

Sixth, activist churches emphasize compassion and advocacy on behalf of the poor, hungry, homeless, imprisoned, or others who may be unjustly treated in society. They may become activist in a number of ways, like Jesus cleansing the temple, in order to prevent people from being neglected or marginalized, oppressed or persecuted, injured violently or killed.

Seventh, charismatic churches emphasize how God uses spiritual gifts for helping Christians manifest their full potential. Spiritual gifts also empower ministry to people inside and outside churches. Pentecostal churches have increased dramatically, and all churches have been influenced by their emphasis upon the presence and power of the Holy Spirit at work today.

Other spiritual traditions could be mentioned: ecumenical, family-oriented, and environmental. There may be no end to spiritual traditions that might develop, but the aforementioned churches represent some of the longstanding ways that Christians have understood the nature of spirituality, personal growth, and effective ministry.

How Does One Decide?

Churches may not resemble just one tradition of Christian spirituality. Instead they may represent two or more emphases, or one emphasis may be primary, while others are secondary. In my opinion, what is important to remember is that all these traditions of Christian spirituality have biblical precedence, and thus may be confidently used.

It is the right and privilege of churches to decide for themselves, in response to God's leading, which spiritual practices and ministries that they will emphasize. However, problems arise when churches disparage and possibly denounce other traditions, mostly because they differ from their own tradition. Although churches may prefer some traditions over others, it is biblically naïve and judgmental when they seem to spend more time criticizing other Christians, rather than spend time promoting their own understanding of spirituality and ministry. Sadly, Christians are sometimes known more for who they hate than for who they love.

Christian Perfection

Does God expect people to become perfect? This question looms in the background whenever we talk about spiritual growth. Christians have differed over the centuries with regard to some of the dramatic exhortations made in Scripture. For example, in the Sermon on the Mount, Jesus said: "Be perfect, therefore, as your heavenly Father is perfect" (Matthew 5:48). At first glance, this exhortation seems impossible. Consequently, some Christians have seen it more as a goal than as an achievable state, or that it refers to a future life, rather than the present. Other Christians, however, take Jesus' exhortation very seriously, believing that God's grace is more powerful than the power of sin, or even of Satan.

Historically, most Christians have been hopeful with regard to how they may and indeed ought to grow spiritually, into greater Christ-likeness. After all, to what would a perfect God lead converts, other than to perfection? Thus, in church history, Christians have talked about saints, deification, beatific vision, mystical union, entire sanctification, Christian perfection, and so on. These terms sound intimidating, especially to those of us who fall far short of perfection! Yet, Christians have always been hopeful that—by God's grace—we may grow in Christlikeness. We may grow in faith, in hope, and in love. Some terms that Christians use seem fantastic and unattainable, and yet they believe that God's grace gives hope for becoming more perfectly loving towards God, others, and even oneself.

For these reasons, hope represents a Christian virtue along with faith and love. Christians are hopeful that they are never alone. The effects of sin are never greater than divine grace, and so they have hope for overcoming that which tests them, personally and socially, spiritually and physically. God's grace does not extend only to private spiritual matters. On the contrary, Christians believe that God is greater than all that besets them, as they partner with God's Holy Spirit in overcoming life's challenges.

Final Comments

I was greatly encouraged to discover the varieties of Christian spirituality. It was not an excuse to be spiritually lackadaisical, picking only the easiest spiritual practices, exercises, or disciplines. On the contrary, learning about family and studious spiritualities were liberating to me personally. They helped me to excel in how I showed my love to others through my primary ways of growing spiritually and of ministering to others, including my children and students.

Knowing that there are so many ways that Christians, historically and today, go about living and promoting spiritual formation, I encourage people to experiment. Learn about other traditions of Christian spirituality, and perhaps try one or more spiritual practices, exercises, or disciplines. You do not need to do all of them, of course! That would be impractical, and perhaps immoderate. However, with the prompting of the Holy Spirit, you will find new ways of being spiritual, of growing, and of ministering that are both pleasing to God and fulfilling to you.

No Holiness but Social Holiness

When I was a senior in high school, my Aunt Naomi asked if I participated in a small group Bible study. I said no, and also that did not know that such groups existed. She encouraged me to get together with a couple of friends, which I did. It was life changing! Even though none of us were all that biblically literate, we learned and grew together in many ways — as friends and as Christians. It was the first of many small groups with which I have been involved in life, and they have been among the most influential experiences I have had in growing spiritually and as a person.

John Wesley once said that there is 'no holiness but social holiness.' Although he was also involved in social activism, Wesley's statement had to do with how the Christian life and spiritual formation best occur in community with others. In addition to church attendance, Wesley coordinated an effective network of mid-week Christian gatherings (called Methodist Societies), class meetings (with groups of men and women who met separately), and small bands of individuals dedicated to holding one another accountable — spiritually, morally, and in service to others.

Since the first century, churches became the primary meeting place of Christians, even though the meetings were informal, being held in people's homes or safe public places, in order to avoid possible persecution. Over time, churches grew, developed institutional structures, and expanded Christian beliefs, values, and practices. Although one might romantically long for emulating life in the early church, it is impossible to do so, given the different socio-cultural contexts in which we live today. In fact, contemporary Christians who claim to imitate the first-century church, claiming to be 'Bible Christians,' have an uncritical view of biblical teachings and are naïve about church history. So much of what Christians today affirm is inextricably bound up with centuries of church traditions, doctrinal formulations, and liturgical practices. The canon of Scripture itself is a product of church decision-making, dependent upon the authority of church leadership and tradition.

So, in talking about 'no holiness but social holiness,' I want to begin by talking about the church. Although it is impossible to present a history of its development, I can focus upon some key concepts that arose among Christians in order to emphasize the importance of the church in representing Jesus and his gospel to the world. Taken together, the church refers to all Christians, and so its witness — good or bad — is the witness of all Christians, in their various manifestations past and present, near and far.

Development of the Church

Scripture talks about the church (Gk., *ekklesia*) as the collective followers of Jesus and of his gospel. It is not clear whether Jesus intended the church to become separate from Judaism, or whether it was to serve as a renewal movement within Judaism. Whatever Jesus' intentions regarding institutional religion, it is clear that Jesus desired for people to be together in community. As Jesus says in the Gospel of Matthew, "For where two or three are gathered in my name, I am there among them" (Matthew 18:20). The church emerged as the place where Christians met weekly, devoting themselves to the instruction of the apostles, fellowship, breaking of bread (an allusion to early sacramental practices), prayer, praise, and distribution of their finances equitably to those in need (see Acts 2:42-47). In time, churches and groups of churches organized themselves, as needed, though no consensus emerged with regard to specifics about administrative structure. Although churches (and later denominations) appeal to Scripture in formulating their self-identity, churches developed distinctively in different places and times, and continue to do so today.

A major transformation of churches occurred in the fourth century, after Emperor Constantine legalized Christianity. Soon thereafter Christianity became the dominant religion in the Roman Empire. This had positive and negative effects. On the positive side, Christians could publicly develop the church, including its doctrines and ministry practices, no longer being social pariahs. On the negative side, the church grew exponentially in size, prestige, and power, which was quite different from the sometimes persecuted gathering of believers that it previously had been.

Debate continues with regard to the long-lasting effects upon the church's religious domination, at least, in Western civilization. Has its dominance caused as much, or more, pain and suffering, than it has relieved pain and suffering? I like to think that it has done more healing than harm. However, if Christians are oblivious to (or in denial about) potential harm that churches do, then they are doomed to harm more people than heal them. Western Christians have been especially ignorant, too often, intentionally ignoring the spiritual as well as socio-cultural, political, economic, and military devastation that churches have caused upon Eastern and Southern countries. In the Middle Ages the church became an empire, much like the Roman Empire that the early Christians feared more than anything else. Yes, the gospel has been proclaimed, but Christians need to have greater awareness, empathy, and fairness in how they treat those outside their immediate tribe, church, and country.

Marks of the Church

Ancient creeds described the church, or true church, as having four marks. For example, you may or may not be familiar with the words of the Nicene Creed: "we believe in one holy catholic and apostolic church." One, holy, catholic (or universal), and apostolic—what do these four marks mean? First, under the lordship of Jesus, there is one church. Second, those who are a part of it are holy, not because of their own holiness, but because of the holiness of Jesus bestowed upon them. Third, the church is catholic, or universal, in the sense that it is intended for all people, regardless of their race, ethnicity, gender, class, language, nationality, sexual orientation, or prior religious affiliation. Fourth, the church is thought of as apostolic—that is, following in the tradition of the first apostles, or followers, of Jesus.

The term apostolic became problematic for subsequent Christians for a couple of reasons. First, when the Roman Catholic Church and Orthodox Churches separated in the eleventh century, both claimed to have the only uninterrupted succession of church authority derived from the first apostles, passed on by the laying on of hands whenever a bishop, priest, or deacon is ordained. Second, when the Roman Catholic Church and Protestants separated in the sixteenth century. Protestants claimed that the only true succession pertained to fidelity to the *teachings* of the first apostles, rather than to a successive ordination of bishops and popes. In other words, Protestants view the church as apostolic in terms of a continuous teaching, rather than a continuous line of leaders.

Protestants did not establish formal "marks" of the church, but two characteristics became representative of the Reformation. First was the right administration of the churches' sacraments, since Protestants thought that Roman Catholic practices had strayed from biblical teachings, relying too much on the rites and rituals of the church sacraments, rather than upon faith. Second was the proclamation of Scripture through preaching, especially doing so in vernacular languages that lay people could understand (notably, the preaching and mass at Roman Catholic Churches at the time was done completely in Latin). In both instances, religious authority was placed primarily in the teachings of Scripture, rather than in the centuries of papal and magisterial teachings of the Roman Catholic Church.

Sacraments: Specific Means of Grace

One of the biggest differences between Roman Catholic and Protestant churches is the role of the Sacraments. Sacraments are often described as outward and visible signs of inward and spiritual divine grace, attended by rites and rituals that developed in church history. The sacraments are thought to be special or specific means of grace, in contrast to general means of grace discussed earlier (for example: prayer, worship). Catholics identify seven sacraments: Baptism, Confirmation, Eucharist, Reconciliation, Anointing of the Sick, Ordination, and Matrimony. Orthodox Christians generally accept these sacraments, calling them 'holy mysteries.' Those who partake of the sacraments receive divine grace *ex opera operato* (Lat., 'from the work worked'), which effect temporal as well as eternal blessings.

Protestants rejected Catholic sacramentalism, thinking it put too much emphasis upon the mediating role of the church, priests, and sacraments, rather than upon the faith of individuals. Instead Protestants most believed that the sacraments were more of a sign (or symbol) of divine grace, and that people's faith should be emphasized, rather than the rites and rituals performed. Protestants tended to recognize only the two sacraments of Baptism and

Eucharist (or Communion, Lord's Supper), believing that they represented the only religious practices plainly instituted by Jesus.

Regardless of the particular view that Christians have about the sacraments, all believe that God continues to work in their lives. Sacraments serve as important ways of remembering how God has worked for their salvation in the past, through the life, death, and resurrection of Jesus, and how God continues to work in assuring, encouraging, and strengthening Christians. The sacraments represent a vital way through which God's Holy Spirit works in and through those who believe, but they are not the only way.

How do we make sense of the sacraments today? Christians may get in arguments about the sacraments — are there seven sacraments, as in the Roman Catholic Church? Or are there two, as in Protestant Churches? Rather than getting hung up on these numerical arguments, it's helpful to go back to the definition of a sacrament mentioned at the beginning of this section: "outward and visible signs of inward and spiritual divine grace." The goal of the sacraments is always to point towards God's grace. God's grace is the most important thing, whether churches practice seven sacraments, two sacraments, or reject the use of the word "sacrament" entirely.

Ecumenical and Interfaith Relations

Churches are often known more for their schismatic tendencies to divide, rather than to work for unity. This is a shame, since Jesus hoped that his disciples remain unified. In John 17:11, Jesus prayed:

> And now I am no longer in the world, but they are in the world, and I am coming to you. Holy Father, protect them in your name that you have given me, so that they may be one, as we are one.

Church leaders such as Willem Visser't Hooft have talked about three ways, at least, that Christians may unify: 1) church merger; 2) doctrinal agreement; and 3) cooperation in ministry. Since the turn of the twentieth century, more emphasis has been placed upon ecumenism (from Gk. *oikonomía*, 'managing a household'), that is, ways for Christians to become more unified. Some churches have merged, and some doctrinal agreements have developed, receiving widespread endorsement, for example, the Lausanne Covenant and Lima Document. The Lausanne Covenant was adopted by the First

International Congress on World Evangelization in 1974, and the Lima Document, also known as "Baptism, Eucharist and Ministry" (BEM), was adopted by the World Council of Churches in 1982.

Most ecumenical activity has occurred through cooperation in ministry, whether it be more focused on social ethics (e.g., World Council of Churches, National Council of Churches) or evangelization and missions (e.g., World Evangelical Alliance, National Association of Evangelicals). These are modest starts, and yet I encourage Christians and churches to focus more upon what unites than upon what divides them, especially for the sake of cooperation in ministry.

As the world grows smaller, so to speak, increased concern has arisen over how to relate with people of other faiths, of other religions. Historically, emphasis was placed upon evangelization, more than anything else. But are there other ways that Christians ought to relate with those from other religions? In loving one's neighbor as oneself, it is incumbent upon Christians to get to know their neighbors, to understand and appreciate their differences, even if they are not persuaded by them. Having conversations with people of different faiths could even be seen as a spiritual practice, which leads believers into deeper reflection about their knowledge and understanding of God.

In addition, people of all religious traditions would do well in standing up for religious freedom, rejecting violence against people of any faiths, regardless of where one lives around the world, and to promote justice and care for the poor, which are values to which all religions agree. If evangelization occurs, one way or another, then so be it. However, relations with other religions ought not to sponsor manipulative methods of evangelization, oppressive political policies, terrorist practices, or militaristic subjugation.

Final Comments

If you want to grow spiritually, and especially if you are not sure about how to do it, then consider getting together with likeminded individuals, whether it be in a church, small group, or one-on-one with a trusted person in whom you have confidence as a friend and spiritual support. Likewise, if you want your witness to have a greater impact upon the world — spiritually and physically, individually and collectively—then it would behoove you to find Christian communities in which you may organize and enhance your effectiveness.

Although there are many places you could choose to go, attending church is a great place to start! Attend one you like, no matter what the reasons are that make the church appealing to you. Churches are not out of date, nor are they irrelevant; they are the people of God for the mission of God in the world. Scripture suggests that just showing up in church, so to speak, serves as a means of grace by which you as well as others may grow in faith, hope, and love, along with receiving other benefits that God desires for you to have.

Priesthood of Believers

When I grew up, I did not know that any Christian churches prohibited women from serving in positions of leadership. My church always had women speakers, evangelists, and missionaries speak in church. In fact, my Aunt Naomi became an ordained minister in my church's denomination, and she was a role model for me, both in Christian practice and in preaching. I was always encouraged by her knowledge of Scripture and passionate sermons.

After leaving home to attend college, I started to attend a large non-denominational church. At one point, I noticed that the pastor stood beside a woman in the pulpit as she shared at length about some ministry program. After church, I asked someone about why the pastor stood there, since it must have been tiring for him to stand beside the woman, since he contributed nothing to her sharing. I was informed that women could not stand alone in the pulpit and speak to the congregation with men present. I came to learn about the church's policies about how men are to give leadership in the home, church, and society, and women are to be subservient.

Since I had never questioned the legitimacy of women in leadership, I began to study Scripture for myself, and over the years, I read a couple of Christian books on the topic. It was not an easy topic to study, but the biblical and other evidences convinced me that leadership among men and women is shared, rather than limited. This includes leadership in marriage, church, and society. Of course, the church of my youth was better in theory, than it was in practice, with regard to empowering women. After my Aunt Naomi retired from more than a quarter-century of missionary work in the Philippines, she could not find a pastoral placement when she returned to the United States. Eventually, Aunt Naomi had to plant a church in order to continue in full-time ministry, which she served until her retirement.

There are many ways that churches minister, and there are many ways that Christians serve in those ministries. Let us look at some of the ways that they have ministered, mostly in service to

God and others, though neither churches nor Christians are perfect. Not yet! But there are observable trajectories that are discernable about ministry in church history. So, it is good for us to look at some of its developments.

Developments in Church Ministry

The first century church was led by Jesus' twelve disciples and other apostles, such as Paul. Gradually deacons were added to fulfill a broader ministry among church members, and to the community. As an increasing number of Gentiles converted to Christianity, it was necessary for councils and elders to represent the church (e.g., Acts 15). Over time, elders and bishops, who oversaw churches in broader geographical areas, served as the primary leaders in the growing churches.

In subsequent centuries, it was not possible for churches to organize expansive ministries, due to recurrent persecution, along with other challenges of living in the ancient world (e.g., communication, transportation). Elders represented local congregations, while bishops oversaw ever increasingly large areas. But the ministry was done as much or more by the laity — the majority of Christians who are not ordained — who influenced family, friends, and those with whom they worked. After Constantine changed the status of churches in the fourth century, and eventually Christians became the dominant religion of Western society, rather than a minority group, ministry was done more and more by ordained clergy, rather than by the laity.

All Are Ministers

At the time of the Reformation, Protestants such as Luther wanted to return ministry more to the laity, arguing that all people are ministers. I Peter 1:9 describes the church — all true believers — as "a chosen race, a royal priesthood, a holy nation, God's own people, in order that you may proclaim the mighty acts of him who called you out of darkness into his marvelous light." Luther said that all Christians are called to minister, and he exhorted church members to contribute in ministry to people, both inside and outside the church. Christians may be called to many vocations, though not necessarily to church leadership. For example, Christians may be called to the vocation of being a business person, laborer, homemaker, or some other work not immediately related to churches. Luther still believed that certain Christians were called by God into full-time or formal ministry positions, which he referred to as the office of pastoral ministry. But these pastoral leaders needed to empower the laity for ministry as well as to minister themselves.

Some Protestant churches, known as "low church" traditions, tend to put more emphasis upon the congregational nature of church organization and leadership, calling and ordaining their own pastors. The term "congregational" suggests that each church congregation is an independent, self-organized group of people. Worship services tend to be simple, including a focus upon biblical preaching and teaching, along with music and singing. By contrast, so-called "high church" traditions tend to put more emphasis upon formal ordination practices, a highly organized church structure, and rich liturgy. Worship services tend to be more elaborate, possibly with processions, vestments (i.e., church-specific clothing, some of it very formal), and prescribed prayers, in addition to biblical preaching and teaching, along with music and singing.

One way of looking at the difference between "low church" and "high church" Christianity is thinking about what is the climax in the church service. In more low church settings, the climax is the sermon, which is often thirty minutes or longer. High church settings, by contrast, can have sermons that are only around ten minutes. The climax of high church services is not the sermon but rather the ritual, most often the eucharist (also known as communion or mass). Low church settings, by contrast, may only have communion about once a month or once a quarter. A small number of Protestant churches have no ordained ministers, relying upon lay leadership for managing church life, worship services, and ministry.

Over the centuries, churches worldwide have increasingly emphasized that ministry needs to be done by all Christians, and not just a select few called to full-time ministry. Certainly, there need to be leaders, but they are to be leaders who empower others to minister where they live among family, friends, work colleagues, and beyond.

Variety of Christian Ministries

Sometimes ministry is described as the *missio Dei* (Lat., "mission of God"). However, is God entirely responsible for ministry to occur, or does God enlist churchgoers to minister as well? Certainly, it is God who ultimately gives the growth, increase, and success of every ministry. But the *missio Dei*, in addition, implies the sending out of Christians for the sake of ministry to others. What kind of ministry or ministries should they do?

Just as Christians have emphasized a variety of understandings of Christian spirituality, they have also emphasized a variety of understandings of ministry. Does this mean that Christians are divided, alienated, and hopeless? Although we might be tempted to say that these descriptions are apropos, they are not. Some church schisms have indeed been caused by sinful reasons; perhaps, too many. But some church differences are sensible, including their ministry emphases. The apostle Paul describes the church as a body, having many parts, all of which reflect different functions, and yet are important to the whole life and ministry of the church (see Romans 12:3-8).

Some church differences reflect multi-cultural, multi-racial, multi-linguistic, and multi-national reasons. H. Richard Niebuhr wrote *The Social Sources of Denominationalism*. Although one may not agree with all of his conclusions, Niebuhr perceptively pointed out how social factors influence churches. Social factors contribute to our understanding of how churches are formed, grow, decline, divide, and unite. So, Christians would do well to focus on social factors, as well as spiritual factors, when thinking about their churches, how to minister effectively to those inside churches, and how to minister effectively to those outside churches.

Ordination of Church Leaders

The religious formalization of pastoral church leadership has generally been known as ordination. Catholic, Orthodox Church, and Anglican traditions consider ordination as a sacrament — Holy Orders. Those called to ordained priesthood in Roman Catholic Churches are expected to take vows of poverty, chastity, and obedience, and so they do not marry. Orthodox and Anglican Churches permit their priests to marry. To a certain extent priests are believed to act in place of Christ — *in persona Christi*. This is why priests alone are allowed to perform the mass in high church settings. They are reenacting the sacrifice of Jesus in the ritual of breaking bread and sharing wine. This view of priesthood as acting *in persona Christi* has the unfortunate consequence of giving the impression that only priests can have access to God. In reality, this is far from the case! Many people who belong to these Christian traditions value the role of the priest, while also affirming peoples' direct access to God in prayer. However, the role of priest is not only theological, it is also structural. These churches tend to have a hierarchical structure where priests are overseen by bishops, perhaps even archbishops. In the Roman Catholic Church, the highest church authority resides in the Pope, a religious position that developed in the ancient church.

Most Protestant churches have some form of ordination, though they may not always use that precise phraseology. Usually some sense of divine calling is expected by those who pursue ordination, but candidates need to go through a period of discernment. Churches, whether they be local or denominationally affiliated, need to confirm the calling that individuals believe they have. So pastors are not ordained without the communal confirmation of churches, believing that they all act in accordance with the leading of God's Holy Spirit. The word "pastor" comes from the Latin word for shepherd, which is a term that Jesus used to describe his ministry during his lifetime (John 10:11). So, in a similar way to priests, pastors are also supposed to be acting in the role of Jesus. However, pastors are generally thought of as leaders of a church, without the extra symbolism of acting "in persona Christi."

Character of a Priest, Minister, Pastor

Every church and denomination has character expectations of those called to be ordained as a priest, minister, or pastor. Some expectations are rigorous, while others are less so. Common biblical passages to which churches turn in evaluating the character of ordained leaders are 1 Timothy 3 and Titus 1. In these passages, church leaders are expected to be upright and holy, disciplined, teach, and so on. In addition, they are to have one wife, not be given to drunkenness, have obedient children, and so on. These latter character qualities can be confusing, especially if you take them literally. For example, what does it mean that ordinands are to have one wife? Does it mean that they are not to be polygamous? Does it mean that only men may be ordained? Does it mean that only married men may be ordained, and not men who have never been married or men whose wives have died? Few if any churches interpret these verses so literally, even if they claim to be literal interpreters of Scripture.

Regardless of the particulars expected by ordinands, Christians and churches generally have high expectations for those who lead them. So, the ordination process usually takes a long time, both for the ordinands and churches, to be confident about their decision-making. But just as Scripture has high expectations for those who lead churches, there are also promises of God's help in fulfilling the functions of church leadership, as determined by individual churches and denominations.

Ordination of Women

Both historically and today, most churches and denominations do not ordain women, at least, not to the level of serving as a senior priest, minister, or pastor. Such churches consider the evidence of Scripture to be decidedly in favor of a hierarchical, patriarchal, or what is sometimes called a complementarian view of the relationship between men and women. With regard to the latter, both males and females are thought to complement one another in their respective roles of male leaders and consenting females. This hierarchical view is held by Catholic Churches, along with many Orthodox and Protestant churches worldwide.

However, since the mid-twentieth century, Christians and churches have increasingly valued the gifts, talents, and skills of women, and it drove them back to Scripture in order to consider anew the ordination of women. Consequently, a growing number of Christians and churches have come to believe that Scripture places more emphasis upon the equal relationship between men and women, than upon a hierarchical relationship. Arguments in favor of egalitarianism are not always the same. For example, some argue that the Holy Spirit gives gifts, talents, and skills for ministry, and thus Scripture contains examples of women in leadership, for example, Deborah and Priscilla. Deborah was a judge in the Old Testament, who led over the people of Israel (Judges 4-5), and

Priscilla was a missionary who served with her husband Aquila, whom Paul said both "work with me in Christ Jesus" (Romans 16:3). In addition, many Christian traditions refer to Mary Magdalene as the "apostle to the apostles," since Jesus first appeared to her after his resurrection and directed Mary to proclaim Jesus' resurrection to the apostles. All four Gospels recount the story of Jesus' selection of Mary to give witness about the good news to everyone, including both men and women.

Others argue that women's subservience has more to do with the fall of humanity into sin, rather than to divine order, and that Christians have long worked to overturn the challenges (and curses) due to the fall. So, they should also overturn men's exclusive leadership. Still others argue:

> There is no longer Jew or Greek, there is no longer slave or free, there is no longer male and female; for all of you are one in Christ Jesus" (Galatians 3:28).

Just as Christians have eliminated hierarchical relationships between Jews and Greeks, and free and slave, they should eliminate them between men and women.

Final Comments

I wish that more Christians would become actively involved in ministry—men and women, old and young, trained and untrained, ordained and lay people. Part of the problem has to do, in my opinion, with Christians not knowing all the legitimate ways that ministry occurs, which have not always been adequately recognized as ministry. For example, consider helping with the practical upkeep of a church facility, which is as important as the church programing; advocating against civil policies or laws that treat people unjustly; showing hospitality to strangers, or those too often neglected in churches as well as society; donating charity for helping people's financial, health, and educational needs. The aforementioned expressions of love are as important to biblical church life as are other mission-oriented ministries.

There are many ways to minister, and perhaps only our imagination limits us with regard to what individual Christians and churches collectively may do in tangibly demonstrating love to their neighbors. Ministry, in its most basic form, means "to serve"—to live your life for others, and not just yourself. Ministry includes all who believe, and it takes physical as well as spiritual forms, individual acts of love as well as collective acts. Christians ought to be creative in how they envision their place in loving their neighbors as themselves!

The Problem of Hypocrisy

No one likes a hypocrite. We have all met them! They include friends or neighbors who criticize you, while you know that they are guiltier of their criticisms than you are. Hypocrites include parents or siblings who obsess over the minutest failing in your relationship with them, while you know firsthand that they are insufferably worse about those failings than you are. They include politicians who denounce governmental decisions and expenditures, when they are not in power, and yet they are duplicitously silent when they are in power and pass the same decisions and expenditures. No one likes a hypocrite!

Regrettably, some of the worst hypocrites exist in churches. They claim to love their neighbor as themselves, and yet they are among the first to say disrespectful or hateful things about others due to their race, ethnicity, sex, class, education, politics, or religious affiliation. Christians can be quick to condemn sexual indiscretions in society and among politicians, and yet they are silent or—worse—the chief defenders of unjust sexual aggressions by their senior pastor or political party's leaders. It is a pretentious reflection of tribalism, of course, when people in general and Christians in particular bitterly judge the failings and discretions of others, while defending their tribe from similar or worse transgressions. Their tribes, of course, include their spouses, families, friends, churches, clubs, states, and countries.

How many times have you heard a Christian or church say that they disapproved of or condemned certain beliefs, values, and actions until it affected someone in their tribe—a spouse? Child? Parent? Friend? Church member? Club member? Political party member? Country? Such individuals feel exempt from former disapproval and condemnation, since they claim that their circumstances are different, or that some fakery explains why they do not have to abide by the same rules by which they disapprove of and condemn others. Indeed, they may continue to disapprove of and condemn others, despite the recognizable contradiction of their

171

ethics. One of the ironies of hypocrisy is that it is easier to spot it in others than it is to recognize and acknowledge hypocrisy in oneself.

What Is Hypocrisy?

Hypocrisy has to do with saying and acting one way, and then condemning and discriminating against others for the exact same things. It has to do with claiming the moral high ground, when in fact one transgresses the same moral. Hypocrisy also has to do with outwardly claiming to be, do, or have something, while inwardly knowing it is not true. It is indistinguishable from lying for the sake of pretentiously elevating oneself (or one's tribe) or contemptibly putting down others. From a philosophical perspective, one could say that people are guilty of logical inconsistencies; from a biblical perspective, people are guilty of hypocrisy, which is sin.

Scripture rejects hypocrisy as a vice, that is, as a sinful act. In particular, Jesus was critical of hypocrisy. In his Sermon on the Mount, Jesus famously said the following:

> Do not judge, so that you may not be judged. For with the judgement you make you will be judged, and the measure you give will be the measure you get. Why do you see the speck in your neighbour's eye, but do not notice the log in your own eye? Or how can you say to your neighbour, "Let me take the speck out of your eye," while the log is in your own eye? You hypocrite, first take the log out of your own eye, and then you will see clearly to take the speck out of your neighbour's eye (Matthew 7:1-5).

Jesus spoke plainly about the problem of people judging others for something, when those same people were guilty of the same (or worse) things. The passage suggests that those who judge others need to be extremely cautious, since they may well be guiltier of judgment than those they judge. Moreover, if they are guiltier, then others will soon find out hypocritical they are.

In many ways, Jesus seemed remarkably tolerant and non-judgmental in his interactions with people. There was one notable exception, however, and it had to do with judging the hypocrisy of leaders in general and of religious leaders in particular. Jesus passionately condemned the hypocrisy of the "scribes and Pharisees." In the book of Matthew, an entire chapter contains his excoriation of them. Here is a sampling of Jesus' censure:

But woe to you, scribes and Pharisees, hypocrites! For you lock people out of the kingdom of heaven. For you do not go in yourselves, and when others are going in, you stop them (Matthew 23:13).

Woe to you, scribes and Pharisees, hypocrites! For you cross sea and land to make a single convert, and you make the new convert twice as much a child of hell as yourselves (Matthew 23:15).

Woe to you, scribes and Pharisees, hypocrites! For you tithe mint, dill, and cummin, and have neglected the weightier matters of the law: justice and mercy and faith. It is these you ought to have practised without neglecting the others (Matthew 23:23).

Jesus acknowledged the need to respect religious leaders. However, respecting the authority of their office does not obligate people to follow their unvirtuous examples. Jesus warned against following their pretentious role models. He said:

The scribes and the Pharisees sit on Moses' seat; therefore, do whatever they teach you and follow it; but do not do as they do, for they do not practise what they teach (Matthew 23:3).

Jesus understood how bad hypocrisy is, and how its unjust effects increased (exponentially?) among those with power. Many people have power, of course, and not just religious leaders. Parents have power over children, and hypocrisy can have oppressive effects upon children. Teachers have power over students, and hypocrisy can have oppressive effects on students. Employers have power over employees, and hypocrisy can have oppressive effects on employees. Presidents, politicians, and the military have power over a country, and hypocrisy can have oppressive effects on the country, and sometimes on the world as a whole.

Hypocrisy and Churches

One of the most common reasons given by people for avoiding church attendance is hypocrisy. It is not the only reason, of course, for why people dislike churches, but survey after survey attest to it. In response, I hear Christians say that the critiques of hypocrisy are unwarranted. They are not the hypocrites, they retort; instead, the people who call Christians hypocritical are the true hypocrites. Fake news, they say! This lame excuse is itself hypocritical, however, since it refuses to consider realistically and empathetically reasonable misgivings that people have about churches. Does not loving our neighbor as ourselves require actually listening to their questions, concerns, and critiques?

The old joke, of course, is that people claim to love Jesus but not the church: "I like Jesus; it's his followers I can't stand!" Regardless of whether we accept these critiques, the fact remains that many people do not attend church, and understandably so, due to Christian hypocrisies. I have attended church all of my life, and I personally recall examples of hypocrisy that provoked grief, if not indignation. In my experience, churches gave pastors (those with power and prestige) a pass for their sexual and financial transgressions, while the same churches shunned others guilty of the same immoralities. Divorce was anathema in churches, until too many in the congregation divorced, and then it ceased being an *inside* concern, except for the indignation that church folk had against divorces and divorcees in *outside* society. People in church sometimes married, divorced, and remarried numerous times. In fact, it seemed that the greater sin was to remain single, and so Christians continually remarried in order blend in, lest they become subject to social ostracism or salacious gossip. Nationwide surveys have demonstrated that the rate of divorce by Christians — regardless of whether they are Protestant or Catholic, liberal or conservative — differs little from unchurched people. So, how can churches demonstrably justify their self-righteous claims about being the champions of marital values?

What are other areas of hypocrisy? Are Christians hypocritical if they condemn premarital sex outside of marriage, until they have a daughter who becomes pregnant and then accept and love her? Are Christians hypocritical if they condemn abortion, claiming to be pro-life, and yet advocate for capital punishment, war, and torture, and refuse to support public healthcare for disadvantaged newborns? Are Christians hypocritical if they reject women's choice for abortion, and yet they affirm women's choice for abortion in cases of rape or incest, or who affirm women's choice for *in vitro* fertilization that usually results in the destruction of unused fertilized embryos? Are Christians hypocritical if they condemn gay sexuality, until they have a brother who acknowledges that he is homosexual and then accept and love him? Are Christians hypocritical if they claim to care for the poor, but refuse to do anything for them — privately or publicly, ecclesiastically or governmentally — claiming that "God helps those who help themselves" or that everyone must "lift themselves up by their bootstraps"? Are white Christians hypocritical if they claim to love their neighbor as themselves, and then caricature black or brown-skinned people, marginalize them, and refuse to hire them, serve them, or even sit next to them? Are U.S. Christians hypocritical if they piously quote Bible verses about welcoming foreigners, but claim that such verses only apply to legally documented foreigners? Are Christians hypocritical if they make daily decisions based on meteorological science, and then they deny climate evidence when it conflicts with their financial or political self-interest? Are Christians hypocritical if they claim that their political party, candidate, or president is God-ordained, and thus exempt from sexual dalliances, financial lawbreaking, foreign subversion, and unconstitutional cover-ups? After all, is it not true that God is neither a Democrat nor a Republican?

In the same chapter that Jesus warned people against one-sidedly judging others, he also said that you know people by the fruit of their actions. In Matthew 7:15-20, Jesus says:

> Beware of false prophets, who come to you in sheep's clothing but inwardly are ravenous wolves. You will know them by their fruits. Are grapes gathered from thorns, or figs from thistles? In the same way, every good tree bears good fruit, but the bad tree bears bad fruit. A good tree cannot bear bad fruit, nor can a bad tree bear good fruit. Every tree that does not bear good fruit is cut down and thrown into the fire. Thus you will know them by their fruits.

Just because people claim to be Christian or to speak for God, it does not mean that they are truly representing Jesus or biblical beliefs and values. Thus, Christians need to be willing and open to self-assessment, that is, to honestly to evaluate themselves and their tribes, lest they unlovingly and unfruitfully live hypocritically.

Certainly, ethical issues are extremely complex. I cannot begin to talk about all the dynamics involved with injustices due to neglect, marginalization, discrimination, oppression, persecution, and violence toward others, and whether Christians resist against *or* comply with them. However, to the non-Christian world, Christians do not seem very consistent in what they say, relative to what they do. Christians in general and Christian leaders in particular are often the butt of comedians' jokes. Alternatively, are comedians' jokes truly religious persecution, or are Christians ashamed about their hypocrisy and flimsy excuses?

Christians need to take harder looks at themselves, and at their churches. They ought not to escape to their various tribes in order to appease their hypocrisies, whether they escape to family, friends, social media, or political propagandists. If people criticize Christians for being hypocritical, then they need to consider those accusations empathetically and critically. Do not just dismiss accusations as being motivated by evil people, political correctness, or Satan. Such motivations may be at work, but that does not excuse Christians from lovingly considering what their neighbors say. If we know how much we dislike hypocrisy in others — the so-called "speck" in their eyes — then why would we dismiss outright the "log" that may be in our own eyes (Matthew 7:3-5), preventing us from flourishing in relationship with God and with others?

Thoughts and Prayers = Be Warmed and Filled?

A common phrase that you may hear from Christians is that, when disasters arise in people's lives, they respond by saying that the grieving people are in their "thoughts and prayers." Politicians and other public figures may also say these words in times of disaster. Now, there is nothing wrong with saying that others are in one's thoughts and prayers. Christians usually do think about those in trouble, and they usually do pray for them. However, the phrase has become clichéd and insincere. Often hearers understand it as an excuse to do nothing for those with problems. When people hear Christians say that people who suffer are in their "thoughts and prayers," they understand the phrase as an excuse by Christians to do nothing for those in need. Too often, Christians' words are received as being vacuous of the kind of compassionate care and social action that they associate with Jesus, rather than with churches. How much evidence can of think of to refute people's criticisms of Christians for being unempathetic and uncompassionate for those "different" from their tribe?

In the book of James, harsh words criticize those people who claim to have lofty beliefs, and yet fail to minister to the tangible needs of people — physically as well as spiritually, collectively as well as individually. James says:

What good is it, my brothers and sisters, if you say you have faith but do not have works? Can faith save you? If a brother or sister is naked and lacks daily food, and one of you says to them, "Go in peace; keep warm and eat your fill," and yet you do not supply their bodily needs, what is the good of that? So faith by itself, if it has no works, is dead (James 2:14-17).

James argues strongly that it is not sufficient to share theoretical words of encouragement—that is, "keep warm and eat your fill"—without practical actions to back them up. Such words to be warm and filled sound hollow, sanctimonious, and hypocritical. James reminds us that love involves tangible ministry for people's physical and bodily needs as well as for their spiritual and eternal needs. In fact, James claims that failure to care both for people's physical and bodily needs casts doubt on the authenticity of one's faith.

Luther did not like the book of James, and he considered it an "epistle of straw." From his perspective, the book had temporal worth but not eternal worth. Luther said this, in part, because he argued against Roman Catholic emphases on good works, advocating instead that people receive eternal by grace alone and faith alone. God does everything, and we do nothing! However, most Christians in church history consider Luther's interpretation of the book of James to be excessive, which is why—in part—he did not remove it from the canon of Scripture. People's cooperation with God's grace, through the Holy Spirit, represents a synergistic cooperation that values people's physical participation and well as spiritual participation. In Scripture, there is no contradiction between the spiritual priorities of faith, hope, and love and the physical priorities of caring for people's needs here and now. Paul, for example, says, "the only thing that counts is faith working through love" (Galatians 5:6). Faith is not inactive, passive, and without applications for temporal life; it is active and loving, compassionately caring for all the needs of people, just as Jesus cared holistically for people to whom he ministered.

Final Thoughts

Christians should listen to and consider seriously accusations about hypocrisy. To ignore such criticisms or to argue glibly that their good works outweigh their less-than-good works is hypocrisy, to be sure. Christians like to say that they are saved by grace, and that they are not yet perfect—in theory. However—in practice—they need to be more careful about not acting pretentiously, sanctimoniously, and hypocritically.

Humility is a Christian virtue, which other ancient people did not acknowledge before the time of Jesus Christ. Instead, ancients emphasized the need to act assertively on behalf of one's self-interest (or of one's tribe); it did not matter if others suffered because of it. However, Jesus taught another way—a way of truth, life, and compassion that does not function the way of the world. Of course, humility does not mean thinking less (or not at all) about oneself, but of thinking about oneself realistically, alert about one's relationship to oneself and others as well as to God. In humility, Christians ought to beware of hypocrisy, and to overturn it in their lives and in their churches.

Part Six

"But May Have Eternal Life"

End Times

After the 1967 Arab-Israeli War, also known as the Six-Day War, when modern-day Israel captured all of Jerusalem, doomsday Christians rekindled their apocalyptic expectations for Jesus' imminent return. Jesus is coming! Jesus is coming again! I was a teenager at the time, and I got caught up in the cataclysmic predictions of Armageddon broadcast by itinerant evangelists, movies (e.g., *A Thief in the Night*), music (e.g., *I Wish We'd All Been Ready*), and books such as *The Late, Great Planet Earth*, by Hal Lindsey with Carole Carlson, which suggested that Jesus would return within five to ten years. Well, Jesus did not return, and Christians predicting Jesus' imminent return have been doing so for a very long time.

Scripture itself suggests Jesus' imminent return and the 'end times' or 'end of the world' (Gk., *eschaton*, from which we derive the study of eschatology). Near the end of his eschatological discourse on the Mt. of Olives, Jesus said: "Truly I tell you, this generation will not pass away until all these things have taken place" (Matthew 24:34). Several times in the New Testament, biblical authors had to ease the enthusiasm (or disappointment) of Christians, since Jesus had not yet returned, that is, his *parousia* (Gk., 'coming,' 'arrival') or 'second coming.'

Throughout church history, numerous Christians believed that they lived in the end times. For example, some Crusaders thought that they were ushering in God's kingdom, and Luther and Calvin believed that they were living in the eschatological last days. Plentiful Christians have actually predicted specific dates for which they prepared for Jesus' return. For example, William Miller spectacularly predicted Jesus' return, or Advent, on October 22, 1844. When Jesus did not return, Miller's Adventist followers experienced a 'Great Disappointment,' but such failed predictions have occurred repeatedly throughout church history, including failed predictions occurring in the twenty-first century.

Everyone would like to know the future, and that desire seems especially intense among Christians who believe that they have special insight into predicting the future. There may even be a smugness about having secret knowledge, since they look forward to the validation of their eschatological beliefs, values, and practices. They would love to have their secret knowledge come true, humiliating Christians as well as non-Christians who scoffed at their cataclysmic speculations about the gloom and doom soon to come.

Ironically, or tragically, Jesus warned his followers about speculating with regard to the future end times. In the same speech on the Mt. of Olives mentioned above, Jesus said:

> But about that day and hour no one knows, neither the angels of heaven, nor the Son, but only the Father…. Therefore you also must be ready, for the Son of Man is coming at an unexpected hour (Matthew 24:36, 44).

In other words, Jesus recommended that his followers should be more focused on being just, righteous, and living here and now, rather than upon speculating about the future.

Apocalyptic Literature

Scripture contains writings known as apocalyptic literature, from the Greek word *apokalypsis* ('revelation'), which is a genre of prophetic writing about God's future dealings with humanity and the world. The book of Revelation contains the most apocalyptic literature in Scripture, but other books are also thought to contain prophecies about the end times, for example, parts of the books of Isaiah, Daniel, Joel, and Zechariah. It's also important to note that apocalypitc literature isn't unique to the Bible. People were writing other apocalyptic texts in other cultures at the same time. It is a genre—much like how "science fiction" and "historical romance" are genres. How should apocalyptic literature be interpreted? Does its genre require a special approach to understanding its meaning?

I have always appreciated four pieces of advice given by Shirley Guthrie, Jr., about what is going to happen to us in the future. He says:

> We must not want to know too much.
> Biblical language about the future is symbolical.
> There is no one consistent biblical picture of the future, but a development in its thought.
> The best insight we have into what God will do is found by looking at what God has done.

First, Guthrie cautions against the human desire to know (or speculate) about every possible detail in the future, since it may lead to a fixation that is neither biblical nor healthy for us, personally and socially as well as spiritually. Certainly, this kind of fixation leads to the criticism of Christians that they are too heavenly minded to be of any earthly good.

Second, despite allusions to real life places, both past and present, biblical language about the future is primarily symbolic. Great care and restraint must be used in discerning what apocalyptic literature is and is not addressing. Even the most self-described literal interpreters of apocalyptic literature claim that such literature is filled with symbolic meaning. For example, vast amounts of theological and popular Christian literature have been written about the meaning of the book of Revelation's references to a beast(s), mark of the beast, false prophet, whore of Babylon, dragon, Gog and Magog, and so on. An expansive cottage industry of fictional writings has arisen about the end times, for example, Tim LaHaye and Jerry B. Jenkins's *Left Behind* series of books, children's books, and movies, which fuels popular speculation about symbolic meanings in apocalyptic literature.

Third, Scripture progressively reveals information to us, and this includes information about the future. The same is true with regard to what Scripture says about heaven and hell, since most of these teachings appear in the New Testament, rather than in the Old Testament. So attention needs to be given about what it says at any given time, and how later Scripture helps to elaborate or surpass what biblical authors said earlier.

Fourth, readers of apocalyptic literature ought not to get caught up in what may happen in the future as the basis for their present hope. Scripture elsewhere clearly talks about what God has done in the past, especially for people's salvation through the life, death, and resurrection of Jesus. Scripture also talks about how Christians ought to believe, value, and practice Jesus' teachings here and now. The present acts and promises of God should contribute more decisively with regard to hope in our present lives, rather than upon uncertain speculations about the future.

Book of Revelation

What are ways that Christians have understood the book of Revelation, the main deposit of apocalyptic literature? In church history, some took a *historic* interpretive approach, saying that the book has more to do about historical events, broadly understood, than about predicting the future. More specifically, a preterist interpretation (from the Lat., *praeter*, 'past,' 'beyond') says that Revelation pertains to historical events that occurred in the first century. For example, first century Palestine was wracked with political turmoil, and it wasn't uncommon for people to anticipate the end of the world as a relief to their present struggles. Scholars who subscribe to this view suggest that the "beast" that is forecast in the Book of Revelation is actually the oppressive emperor Caesar Nero, whose name when converted into numbers adds up to the sinister number "666" (first century writers were very into numerology, and gave a numeric value to every number of the alphabet).

A futurist interpretation believes that the book of Revelation gives a chronology, more or less, of future world events. The more one studies it, the more one is able to interpret current events and to predict what will happen next. Most of the dramatic eschatological preaching, movies, songs, and books take a futurist approach to apocalyptic literature.

A symbolic, allegorical, or idealist interpretive approach to the book of Revelation says that apocalyptic literature is not about historical events, past or future. Instead they convey theological affirmations about how God ultimately is in control of the world, and that people in general, and Christians in particular, may have hope in the midst of life's trials and tribulations.

Millennialism

Sometimes different views of eschatology, especially about the end times, are categorized in terms of their views about the *millennium* (Lat., "one thousand years"). It is an allusion to a thousand year reign of Jesus on earth mentioned in Revelation 20. Is this a literal future reign, or is it something else? So much of Christian eschatology has to do with how one interprets the Book of Revelation, which provides the greatest amount of apocalyptic literature in Scripture.

Amillennialism became the dominant view in the ancient church, which said that references to the reign of Jesus are symbolic or allegorical. Augustine was a proponent of amillennialism, and this view was prominent among Catholic, Orthodox, and Reformation churches. Most believed that Jesus would indeed come again, as he promised in the Gospels. But the book of Revelation does not contain a chronology of future events.

Postmillennialism arose primarily after the Reformation, and also advocates for a more symbolic or allegorical interpretation of the book of Revelation. Certain Protestants were hopeful that, just as the church was growing due to evangelization and missions, they would progressively bring about God's kingdom on earth. Only then would Jesus return.

Premillennialism believes that Jesus will return, and that apocalyptic literature provides sufficient prophetic content to identify the signs and the times of Jesus' return. Millennialists sometimes argue that they alone believe that Jesus will visibly and physically return, and that their views were marginalized in the ancient church. But amillennialists and postmillenialists also believe that Jesus will visibly and physically return, though they avoid speculating about current and future events.

Premillennialists disagree, however, with regard to the precise time that Jesus will return, and how Christians will rise up or be 'raptured,' which is an allusion to 1 Thessalonians 4:17:

> Then we who are alive, who are left, will be caught up in the clouds together with them to meet the Lord in the air; and so we will be with the Lord forever.

When will this time of 'a carrying off' (from the Lat., *raptus*) occur? Will it be a public or secret event?

Adventists advocated for a post-tribulation rapture, which would be public and victorious. The tribulation generally refers to a seven-year period of worldwide pain and suffering, based upon apocalyptic literature in the books of Revelation and Daniel. Thereafter, Jesus would set up the millennial kingdom. Adventists believe in the imminent return of Jesus, but they expect it to occur after a terrible time of tribulation and divine wrath, which living Christians must endure. Thus, Christians need to prepare themselves for hard times to come, knowing that only God can ultimately bring about the final consummation of the world.

In contrast, dispensationalists advocated for a pre-tribulation rapture, which would be secret and prior to the seven-year period of worldwide pain and suffering. Thereafter, Jesus would return with those who had been secretly raptured, in order to set up the millennial kingdom. Dispensationalists also expect the world to become worse, evidenced by "wars and rumors of wars" (Matthew 24:6) and by "earthquakes...famines and plagues" (Luke 21:11). However, Christians will be secretly removed from earth in dramatic fashion, and all others will be "left behind" (alluding to Matthew 24:40-42).

So-called mid-tribulationists advocated that the tribulation should be divided in half, the first half involving tribulations caused by people and the second half involving the pouring out of divine wrath upon the world. Because God is not thought to punish Christians directly, it is argued, the rapture will secretly remove them before eventually establishing the millennial kingdom. So, a secret rapture will occur; however, it will occur in the middle of the seven years. The first three and a half years involve tribulation, primarily caused by humanity, while the last three and half years involve divine wrath directly meted out by God on those left behind.

Ideas Have Consequences

What Christians believe about the future impacts how they live here and now. Premillennialists, for example, do not think that alternative millennial views promote sufficient urgency, regarding the imminent return of Jesus. From their perspective, Christians ought to evangelize as much as possible, since the world will only become worse until Jesus returns. Postmillennialists think that premillennialists are too negative, not believing that God's grace is sufficient to promote present-day justice as well as evangelization. As such, premillennialists may abandon their God-ordained responsibilities for people's physical and social needs, arguing that only Jesus can make such things right, and so why bother? Amillennialists would say that one cannot accurately predict whether life will become better or worse in the future, but that does not absolve one from caring now for all of people's needs — spiritual and physical, individual and social.

Literalistic oriented approaches to interpreting apocalyptic literature sometimes try to force Jesus' second coming by promoting the fulfillment of prophecies that they believe must first come to pass. For example, some premillennialists believe that the nation of Israel needs to recapture Arab lands, rebuild the temple in Jerusalem, and so on. In order to ensure a fulfillment of prophecies in keeping with their interpretations and expectations, they may promote violence, war, and other atrocities. Many of these people are known as Christian Zionism, supporting Israel 'right or wrong,' without any subjecting their actions to normal Christian ethical analysis. They may also obsess over conspiracy theories having to do with a 'one world order' or accusations about who might be the 'Antichrist,' which is an allusion to biblical passages in 1 John (e.g., 2:18, 22). Lamentably, Protestants have chronically accused Roman Catholic Popes of being the Antichrist, since the time of the Reformation, and more recently Christians have exhibited a penchant to accuse U.S. Presidents (usually of opposing political parties) of being the Antichrist. However, Christians ought to be wary about blind disregard of known laws—biblical and international—for the sake of speculating about prophetic allusions in apocalyptic literature, which may be motivated by power politics, economics, and nationalism more than Scripture.

Final Comments

I think that the overarching theme of apocalyptic literature is hope, despite the presence of tribulations caused by people and the potential consequences of divine wrath. Individually, life may be uncertain and terrible. In fact, for collective groups of people (e.g., racial, ethnic, linguistic, and national groups), life may be terrible as well. Moreover, there may be little that can be done to avoid altogether tribulation and wrath, even for Christians. As people committed to loving God as well as our neighbor, Christians should strive to ease the pain and suffering for all people in the present moment, rather than fixating on the pain and suffering of some distant event.

Christians would do well to be wary of eschatological speculators, especially those who promise the blithe avoidance of future pain and suffering. They do not adequately prepare Christians for the kinds of suffering that Jesus warned his disciples about, or that most New Testament authors warned people about with regard to future discrimination, oppression, and persecution. But all is not lost; there is hope! There is hope for present aid by God, through the Holy Spirit, churches, and other faithful servants, and ultimately there is the blessed hope of eternal life in heaven, in addition to all the benefits that God promises for people here and now.

What About Those Who Do Not Believe?

Over the years, I have asked the questions: What about those who do not believe? What will be their eternal destiny? What about those who lived before the time of Jesus? What about those who have never heard the gospel, or never heard it explained well?

Other questions arise: What about infants who die? What is the eternal destiny of deceased children, who may not have reached an age of accountability (or reason)? What about those deceased people who were mentally, emotionally, or in some other way physically challenged, so that it is difficult to imagine how they can credibly be held accountable spiritually and morally for their decision-making?

Still other questions arise: What about those who die who affirm other religious traditions, other faiths? In particular, what about those who die who were deeply devout and manifested exemplary love for others, as Jesus loved others, and yet did not do so as a Christian?

These questions, and more, are not limited to me. They are questions that many people ask, both inside and outside the Christian tradition. Moreover, these are not academic questions; they pertain to real life people we know — perhaps children, parents, relatives, relatives by marriage, friends, neighbors, coworkers, and more. The proverbial 'shrinking of the world' reminds us again and again that Christianity cannot be conceived only within the narrow context of hegemonic Christian cultures. The world is religiously diverse, both inside and outside the United States, and so all these questions are crucial in talking about the eternal well-being of those who could be called the "unevangelized." Indeed they may be the most important questions we ask, given the likelihood that each and every one of us knows people who are not Christians, who are adherents to another religious tradition, or who just do not fit religious categories with which we grew up.

Complex Biblical Culture

Lest we arrogantly think that our current world situation is too complex for Scripture to be relevant today, we need to remember that biblical authors wrote over many hundreds of years, in multiple nations, with multiple languages, engaging with people of multiple racial, ethnic, cultural, linguistic, and religious backgrounds. Biblical authors were neither ignorant nor unconcerned about the diversity of the socio-cultural world in which they lived.

Of course, Scripture does not specify one particular way of dealing with the varieties of people with whom biblical authors came into contact. Sometimes they were resistant to those who were 'other,' for example, Israelite leaders such as Joshua and Ezra who wanted to safeguard both the religious and ethnic purity of the people of Israel. Other times, biblical authors dealt with the challenges of a growing Christian movement in which more converts were non-Jews than Jews. Some of their responses to the challenges of growing diversity serve as role models for today; other responses were less than exemplary. So, Scripture serves as a relevant starting point for thinking about the eternal destiny of all people, and not just Christians.

Salvation outside Christianity?

Generally speaking, Christians view the so-called unevangelized (or non-Christians) in, at least, three ways. First, the exclusivist view says that no one can be saved who does not explicitly name the name of Jesus as their savior and lord (e.g., John 14:6; Romans 10:9-17). This restrictive view of salvation has probably represented Christianity the most over the centuries, and socio-culturally may have aided in distinguishing itself, vis-à-vis, religious competitors, which were not as exclusivist in their understanding of salvation, enlightenment, or self-actualization.

Second, the pluralist view says that all religions are equally valid, and therefore each religion serves as a way for salvation, enlightenment, or self-actualization. Historically, pluralism has been rejected by most Christians, since it is thought to detract from the unique saving role of Jesus Christ.

Third, various inclusivist views have said that there may be alternative ways complementary to clear teachings in Scripture about salvation, by which the unevangelized may be saved and receive eternal life in heaven. These represent extraordinary means of salvation, as opposed ordinary means (or orders of salvation). *The Westminster Confession of Faith* (1646), for example, talks about the "ordinary possibility of salvation," but does not explicitly rule out the extraordinary possibility of salvation some other way. For example, Vatican II Catholic theologian Karl Rahner proposed that God's salvation may extend to people who live good and sincere lives outside of the church—so-called "anonymous Christians." So, what are some of the inclusivist views that Christians have posited?

Inclusivist Views of Salvation

The most prominent inclusivist view says that Scripture suggests ways that people may be saved, even though they may not know or name the name of Jesus. For example, the apostle Paul says that those who do not have the Old Testament laws are judged by their instinctual obedience or moral conscience, rather than by the law. Paul says:

> When Gentiles, who do not possess the law, do instinctively what the law requires, these, though not having the law, are a law to themselves. They show that what the law requires is written on their hearts, to which their own conscience also bears witness; and their conflicting thoughts will accuse or perhaps excuse them (Romans 2:14-15).

Since God "desires everyone to be saved and to come to the knowledge of the truth" (1 Timothy 2:4), God may excuse people's sins and grant them eternal life, due to extraordinary means of grace. There is no guarantee, of course, that God provides extraordinary means of grace, but biblical evidence suggests that people may be saved in more ways than we ordinarily imagine.

Other Christians argue that God may grant people the chance to accept or reject salvation after death. This postmortem view of evangelization arises from verses that suggest Jesus preached to the unevangelized, after his death. For example, 1 Peter talks about how Jesus "made a proclamation to the spirits in prison," who had lived during the time of Noah (3:19). I Peter continues:

> For this is the reason the gospel was proclaimed even to the dead, so that, though they had been judged in the flesh as everyone is judged, they might live in the spirit as God does (4:6).

Even Jesus said:

'Very truly, I tell you, the hour is coming, and is now here, when the dead will hear the voice of the Son of God, and those who hear will live (John 5:25).

So, biblical evidence suggests that there may be a postmortem opportunity for people to respond to the gospel of salvation if, in this life, circumstances prevented them from hearing it. Again, people ought not to count on the possibility of responding to the gospel after they die, but Scripture does not preclude this so-called 'second chance.'

Still other Christians believe that, in this life, God will miraculously provide people, angels, dreams, or other circumstances that help save those who sincerely desire to be in a right relationship with God, even though they had not previously heard the gospel of Jesus. For example, Scripture talks about several miraculous ways that the gospel was given to people. Acts 8:26-40 tells the story of how Philip was led by an angel in order to evangelize an Ethiopian eunuch, and Acts 10:1-48 tells the story of how the Gentile Cornelius had a vision and received Spirit-led messengers who helped Cornelius be converted by the apostle Peter. If one believes that miracles still occur, then modern day miracles may occur for the evangelization of people previously far removed from hearing the gospel. Missionaries, in fact, tell anecdotal stories about God-fearing non-Christians having their faith affirmed through contact with missionaries, angels, or other extraordinary emissaries of God.

In my opinion, none of these examples of inclusivism, in and of themselves, prove that God provides alternative, extraordinary ways for people to be saved. But there certainly is enough biblical evidence to give people—both Christians and non-Christians—pause about automatically excluding people from salvation and eternal life in heaven, just because they have not explicitly received the gospel message and explicitly named the name of Jesus as their savior and lord. In other words, there is hope for those people, which includes millions and billions of them, who have not heard or were, for whatever reasons, prevented from hearing the Gospel in this life. These inclusivist views suggest that God is not an arbitrary God, who saves and damns people willy-nilly, relative to the unpropitious place, time, and circumstances in which they lived.

Of course, some Christians believe that before the creation of the world, God determined who would be saved and who would be damned. However, this is not the majority view. The majority of Christians believe that God expects some decision-making on the part of people as a condition for their salvation. Although people may not be saved through ordinary orders of salvation, they may be saved through extraordinary ways that take into account their consciences, postmortem opportunities for evangelization, or miraculous means by which all may be saved.

Death of Innocents

What about infants who die, or those who are mentally, emotionally, or in some other way challenged, so that they do not have an informed opportunity to respond to the gospel message of Jesus? There is no consensus among Christians on these issues. Sometimes views are assumed, rather than formally adopted by churches or denominations. Be that as it may, several views have been offered in order to talk about how God treats innocent babies and also people who do not seemingly have the same potential as others to decide for themselves with regard to salvation.

Christians who believe that God predestined the election (and damnation) of people before the creation of the world would appeal to God's sovereignty and mercy with regard to the death of infants. From this perspective, no conditions in this life apply to people's eternal status, and so infants' untimely deaths would not affect God's predestination, though certainly Christians would grieve at the tragic death of any person.

A variation of the aforementioned view involves the concept of God having "middle knowledge," that is, that God both knows about the present world, and about an infinite number of people's possible alternative existences, and the choices that they would make in each one. Based upon this middle knowledge (of counterfactuals, regarding possible alternative existences), God may save people, including infants, based upon decisions in those possible alternative existences, and not necessarily upon the situation they experience in this world. Although this is an intriguing theology, people lack God's middle knowledge, and so they have to make do with what is known about this world, rather than about what is unknown in an infinite number of possible alternative existences.

Christians who have a so-called high view of the sacraments believe that the sacrament of Baptism guarantees that an innocent child who dies will receive eternal life. However, what about those who are not baptized? Catholics sometimes talk about limbo as a liminal existence for unbaptized infants, though it is an unofficial doctrine of the church. Limbo typically is described as a shadowy place, but not a place of punishment. Recently Catholic scholars have emphasized the hope, though not the certainty, that unbaptized infants go to heaven, rather than to limbo.

In practice, many Christians believe that God would never damn infants to hell, just because they died so young, without the opportunity to decide for themselves about the gospel of salvation. But this affirmation is not an official doctrine that Christians and churches generally affirm. Be that as it may, infants (and young children) who die are thought to receive a free pass to heaven, since they never had the opportunity to reach an age of spiritual and moral accountability (or age of reason).

In like manner, those who are mentally, emotionally, or in other ways challenged in their decision-making, are also thought to receive eternal life in heaven. Christians and churches have talked even less about these people — these innocents — who we regularly find amongst ourselves.

One might wonder if there are not many people who, for one reason or another, never reach an age of accountability. Due to circumstances about a person's situatedness with regard to place of birth, cultural background, and religious affiliation, one may wonder if there will be many people who never reach accountability in this life, even as adults. Given the diverse challenges that people experience, we can hope that God will be more empathetic than exclusionary, more merciful than damning.

Final Comments

I like to make a distinction between an 'article of belief' and an "article of hope." I hope that no one suffers in eternity for refusing to humble themselves, repent, and believe in Jesus as their savior and lord. I think that there is sufficient biblical evidence to expect that God will give people as many chances as are necessary to be saved, regardless of the extraordinary means by which that might happen. Likewise, I think that there is sufficient biblical evidence to expect that not everyone will convert — past, present, or future. So be it. It is the risk God took, so to speak, in creating people with freedom of choice, which was necessary for the freedom to love, and to be in relationship with God and with others.

Because I can only look at life in the present, not having the knowledge and understanding that I anticipate having in the future, I think God wants us here and now to continue to proclaim the gospel. Its benefits help us now as well as for eternal life. Salvation, after all, is as much for the well-being of people in this life as it is for the afterlife.

Heaven and Hell

I distinctively remember two times in my life when people asked me the question: What is heaven like? Certainly others have asked me this question, especially in my theology classrooms. But I mostly remember two such instances: The first was Dr. Marvin Karasek, now deceased, who was one of my university advisors, and the second was my then five-year old daughter Heidi.

Dr. Karasek asked me, at one point, what I wanted to do in life. I told him that I wanted to study religion and teach. Dr. Karasek and I had a good relationship, and he kidded me — good naturedly — about Christianity, though his humor had an irreverent edge. At one point he asked why anyone would want to go to heaven, and spend eternity sitting on clouds and strumming harps. I kidded back, saying he watched too many cartoons. Then he asked me what I thought heaven was like. Suspecting he would not like any answer I gave, I said that he should think about his favorite thing in life, and imagine that he would be able to experience it all the time in heaven. Dr. Karasek clapped his hands and said with glee: "Twenty-four hour sex!"

Driving on our way to camp in Yosemite National Park, I remember Heidi sitting beside me in our van. While looking out the window, enjoying the beautiful mountain scenery, she asked what heaven is like. Instead of responding — as teachers are apt to do — I asked what she thought heaven is like. Heidi said: "I think it looks like earth, only better." At the time, I remember being greatly impressed by what she said. Indeed, I learned something from my four-year old daughter because I think that Heidi captured what heaven is like far better than I did as a university student.

The truth of the matter is that we do not really know what heaven will be like. But Scripture assures us that it — along with other promised benefits by God — will exceed our expectations. I have always liked the words of Paul, imagining them to apply to heaven: "But, as it is written, 'What no eye has seen, nor ear heard, nor the human heart conceived, what God has prepared for those who love him,'" alluding most likely to Isaiah 64:4 (1 Corinthians

197

2:9). The descriptions of heaven in Scripture are predominantly symbolic, encouraging our imaginations about the wonderfulness of heaven-like existence and what our relationships there will be.

Biblical Language about Heaven and Hell

It is ironic—and perhaps hypocritical—when some Christians argue vehemently that hell must be viewed literally as consisting of eternal fire, brimstone, and gnashing of teeth. To them, believing otherwise is a sign of being weak on Scripture, divine judgment, and eternal damnation. Yet, when asked about heaven, these same Christians may say that biblical descriptions are just a foreshadowing of good things to come. After all, biblical language in the book of Revelation describes heaven—the "new Jerusalem"—as a cube-shaped city, each side measuring approximately 1,500 miles, with walls more than 200 feet thick, built with gold and precious stones. As appealing as these images of heaven might be to some people, others of us might also like there to be fields and streams, mountains and oceans, cushy couches and soft beds. In other words, most of us do not feel limited by biblical language in imagining how wonderful heaven will be!

So why are people, including Christians, offended if one does not literally use biblical language to describe hell? For example, hell is sometimes described as a place of weeping and gnashing of teeth, bottomless pit, furnace of fire, unquenchable fire, eternal fire, torment forever, no rest day or night. It is also called a place of darkness or black darkness, which does not seem as severe. Yet, all the imagery is intended to say that one ought to avoid it at all costs!

So, what should we think about hell? It depends, in my opinion, on what you think about biblical imagery regarding heaven. If you like the literal imagery of heaven as a place made out of gold and jewels (and no soft sofas, beds, or soft grassy fields by a river), then you will probably like the literal imagery of hell as eternal fire, brimstone, and gnashing of teeth. However, if you take more of a symbolic view of the imagery of heaven, then you need to be content with viewing hell as a place to be avoided at all costs, but not necessarily with a literalistic view of it.

Is hell "below" us as suggested in 2 Peter 2:4? (Is heaven "above" us as suggested in Acts 1:9 and 1 Thessalonians 4:16-17?)

Most Christians don't think that you'll find hell by digging a deep hole in the ground. The spatial language in Scripture used to describe hell (and heaven) is usually thought to be symbolic, rather than geological or astrological. Instead hell and heaven are ultimately thought to be spiritual dimensions, rather than physical dimensions.

Justice of Heaven and Hell

Scripture talks over and over again about final judgment. It does not say precisely what that judgment will be like, but it will be just and as compassionate as possible in deciding the eternal destinies of people. Without judgment, however, there would be no way for justice to win over the many injustices that occur presently in life. People have little problem looking forward to eventual justice for those who, in this life, literally got away with murder, along with discrimination, oppression, and the exploitation of others. They find it more difficult to think that God will hold people accountable for passive indifference to God or for the lack of faith. As difficult as it is for people to comprehend, Scripture says that God knows people's hearts, consciences, and other aspects of their spiritual state so that no injustice will be done to them, based upon circumstances outside of their control (e.g., where they lived, when they lived, and what they knew about God).

Are the very concepts of heaven and hell just? For example, how can a Christian, who claims to be loving, go happily to heaven, knowing that others are damned? After all, did not the apostle Paul say that he would be willing to be accursed in order than his fellow Jews might be saved (Romans 9:3)? Of course, what Paul longed for is not humanly possible, because people's actions and attitudes cannot merit salvation for others, much less themselves. Furthermore, Christians cannot be considered selfish for wanting eternal life, heaven, and a face-to-face relationship with God. Scripture says that people were made for relationship with God, as well as with others, and so they are no more selfish to desire it than they would be considered selfish for wanting to breathe, drink, and eat.

What of hell? Is it just? Why should people suffer for eternity for sins committed temporally in life? In theory, one sin makes a person culpable for eternal damnation. Although this may be true in theory, it trivializes all that Scripture says about justice and justification, about atonement and becoming at-one with God. People receive hell because they choose it, and not because God unreasonably puts them there. I have always liked what C.S. Lewis said about hell, suggesting how God gives people as many chances as are needed to repent and believe, even after death. In the novel *The Problem of Pain*, Lewis said: "I willingly believe that the damned are, in one sense, successful, rebels to the end; that the gates of hell are locked on the inside." In a sense, the existence of hell represents an act of mercy on God's part, since it provides an eternal abode for those who do not wish—and may never wish—to fellowship with God.

Degrees of Reward and Punishment?

Are there degrees of reward in heaven, and degrees of punishment in hell? Scripture surprisingly says quite a bit about both, and various church traditions have talked—in one way or another—about piling up treasures in heaven and multiplying punishments in hell. Although Christians might like the concept of multiplying punishments, especially for the vilest tyrants in history, they usually demur when it comes to the concept of piling up treasures in heaven. Biblical references to storing up "treasures in heaven" have more to do with setting people's present-day priorities—focusing on heavenly things, rather than upon earthly things—and not about an eternal retirement fund (Matthew 6:19-21). For the sake of consistency, one ought not to talk about degrees of punishment in hell, if one does not also talk about degrees of reward in heaven.

Those who are Christians have no reason to fear judgment. Although it may be a time of remembrance and learning, judgment is the time that Jesus' atonement becomes effective for those who have believed, repented, been baptized, and become reconciled with God. It is not because of people's good works or merits that they are saved. That is impossible, but with God, all things are possible. At judgment, Christians receive final absolution for their sins, and become inheritors of eternal life in heaven with God along with others who are saved.

Intermediate State?

What happens after you die? What will you experience? Christians have had a variety of views. It may not seem to be an important question for you now, but for anyone who has had a loved one die — especially someone who died unexpectedly, or who died way too early in life — the question becomes more important, for the sake of grieving, if for no other reason.

Many Christians have believed in an intermediate state, following death, which is how individuals continue to exist, before the final resurrection, judgment, and determination of people's eternal destinies. Some have considered this intermediate state to be like a soul sleep, in which people persist in a kind of unconscious state. Others have considered it to be like disembodied souls or spirits, who exist ghost-like until the end times. Still other Christians think that a separation of the righteous and unrighteous occurs, and they receive a foretaste of heavenly reward and hellish punishment. Creedal references to the 'communion of saints' can be understood as those Christians who have died, and to whom people still living may petition for intercessory prayers by the saints to God on behalf of those who are still alive on earth.

Note that Catholic belief in purgatory represents a place that believers are thought to go, before receiving eternal life in heaven. It is not considered a second chance for salvation. Instead, purgatory is the place after death to which Catholics think that believers go — people who is this life did not live holy lives, and who need to go through a process of spiritual and moral purgation (that is, purification) before receiving eternal life.

Not all Christians believe, however, that there is an intermediate state to which believers go after death. They believe that, when people die, they immediately leave the boundaries of space and time, and are translated before eternal God. Hence, there is not intermediate state. After death, they immediately appear face-to-face before God for judgment.

For Christians, judgment represents the moment of receiving glory, eternal life, and heaven — not because of their worthiness of salvation, but because of the salvation provided for them through Jesus. Just as in life, there will occur growth in knowledge, love, and fellowship in heaven. It will not be a static existence, but a living, flourishing existence of love with one's whole heart, soul, mind, and strength.

Final Comments

Do I look forward to going to heaven? Absolutely! Do I think it will be a place for strumming on harps all day on clouds in worshipping God? No, I think that heaven will be a dynamic place of perpetual growth in heart, soul, mind, and strength, and of flourishing relationships with God as well as with others. Might it be a place for remembering the past? Perhaps, though if it happens, then the end result will be positive, instructive, and constructive, rather than negative.

Will there be a hell? In my opinion, yes; I also think that God gives people as many chances as are necessary to be saved. How that will happen, I cannot say, but Scripture suggests over and over that God is more welcoming than damning. May some never repent and believe? Again, Scripture suggests that this will be the case, and that hell will indeed be a place of mourning and anguish. I also think that the greatest anguish will be due to eternal separation from God. But it will be their choice for being in hell, rather than upon an unfathomable decision by God. This is why right decision-making by us is so important, both for how we base our lives upon love here and now, and for how we hope for eternal life through faith:

For God so loved the world that he gave his only Son, so that everyone who believes in him may not perish but may have eternal life (John 3:16).

Epilogue

John 3:16 was a great verse to start a book about Christianity! It suggests that Jesus welcomes everyone, and gives eternal life for those who choose to believe in him. The passage further suggests that Jesus was not about condemning people. On the contrary, Jesus wants to embrace people, heal them, and help people to flourish—spiritually and physically, individually and collectively.

In addition, John 3:16 serves as a helpful springboard for talking about the whole of Christianity. I talked about God—the nature of God, the existence of God, and the love of God. I talked about creation, humanity, and the predicament they're in due to sin, ignorance, misery, and bondage. I talked about Jesus, the atonement, the Holy Spirit, and how people may decide to accept or reject God's gracious offer of forgiveness, of reconciliation with God, and restoration into the divine image in which they were created.

With regard to the Christian life, I talked about how salvation is not for eternity only. It's also for how we live here and now. Studying Christian beliefs, values, and practices reveals that Scripture talks mostly about how in this life we may live rich, fulfilling lives. Moreover, it talks about how we ought to advocate for justice as well as for justification, and that love should tangibly minister to problems of neglect, marginalization, oppression, and persecution as well as to problems of guilt, shame, and broken relationships.

When you see John 3:16 plastered on billboards or on soda cups or on placards at professional sporting events, you'll no longer have a knee-jerk reaction to it. Instead you'll have an informed and hopefully positive response. John 3:16 can serve as a key to stimulating great thoughts, great living, and of course, great eternity.

Belief, Hope, and Love

After reading this book, you may find reasons to believe in God that you've never considered before. Yes, God exists. It's a matter of faith, and not of rational and empirical argumentation. Such argumentation may help you to believe, or it may help you to understand and communicate your beliefs better. But bottom line is that people have to make a decision about what they trust about Jesus, and about his gospel message. Will you accept it, and entrust your life to it? Or will you reject it, perhaps claiming to be "spiritual but not religious." The latter phrase has become cliché nowadays, and cannot take the place of the most important decision in your life.

There are also many reasons to hope. To be sure, there's reason to hope for eternal life. Throughout the book, salvation represents the blessed hope that all people have due to the atoning work of Jesus' life, death, and resurrection. But the hope of Christianity is also for the present! Just as Jesus cared for the poor, proclaimed release for those held captive, healed those who are blind, and set free those who are oppressed, Christians are to minister enthusiastically in the same ways. Biblical teaching advocates on behalf of those treated unjustly, in addition to treating them with compassion. There ought not to be racism, sexism, classism, and other types of bigotry. Christians ought to be at the forefront of combating injustice in the world, and they absolutely ought not to be the cause of them!

Of course, the book should give readers reasons to love — to love God with one's whole heart, soul, mind, and strength. They should also love their neighbors as they love themselves. Loving oneself is not idolatrous, prideful, or self-serving; it's what God has called us to do. If we don't love ourselves appropriately, then won't our love for others be inappropriate? In the book, I talked about how the primary attribute of God is love. Similarly, God wants people to love broadly and deeply. And God's Holy Spirit aids us in achieving this highest goal, this greatest commandment. Although it sounds cliché, love represents the core of quality relationships, and in the end, that's what's most important in life — our relationships! Maybe now you'll be more inclined to focus on love, and in having love become the overriding concern for all your relationships, including your relationship with God.

What's Next?

In response to John the Baptist's preaching, penitents asked: "What then should we do?" (Luke 3:10). Surprisingly, perhaps, to many Christians, John did not give expected responses, such as telling them to pray, read Scripture, or attend public worship. Instead John told them to do very tangible, justice-oriented things, for example, not to cheat and not to bully. Often people, including non-Christians as well as Christians, have religious expectations about what they should or should not do—expectations that may reflect their personal and socio-cultural background, more than Scripture. After all, thoughtful time spent studying Scripture may actually lead one to act in ways that do not look stereotypically Christian!

People need to be aware of the challenge of bringing together their "theory and practice." In a religious context, this bringing together of people's beliefs and values (theory) with their actions (practice) involves multiple dimensions: spiritual and physical, individual and collective. Matters of both theory and practice influence people's choices to be saved (or to reject God's gift of salvation); they also have to do with how people choose to live here and now. As such, people must decide for themselves—by the grace of God—about who they will be, think, speak, and act.

John 3:16 challenges people, at least, to make one decision. Typically, the decision is thought of in terms of conversion—in believing, repenting, being baptized, and in becoming an obedient disciple of Jesus. I recommend that people ought not to put off this decision to believe in Jesus, if they have not already done so.

It is also important for those who are converts to Christianity to avoid half-baked and half-hearted views of it. John 3:16 is a great place to start in learning about Jesus, Scripture, and the church, but it cannot be the end point. John 3:16 points to a much larger religious understanding, a more welcoming and non-condemning understanding of Jesus' gospel than is often practiced. It has to do with a Christianity that cares about justice as well as justification, loving for those who are impoverished—in poverty's many manifestations—and for reaching out to all in the world who are neglected, marginalized, oppressed, and persecuted.

It is my hope that this book has served to broaden people's understanding about Jesus, about salvation, and about justice-oriented as well as love-oriented Christian living. Furthermore, it is my hope that readers take utmost responsibility in their decision-making, both in accepting Jesus as their savior and lord, and in living in ways that reflect all of Jesus' life and teachings.

Scripture Index

Subject Index

Made in the USA
San Bernardino, CA
07 June 2020